IRONS IN THE FIRE

Irons in the Fire

NOR HALL

Station Hill
of Barrytown

Published by Station Hill of Barrytown, the publishing project of the Institute for Publishing Arts, Inc., 120 Station Hill Road, Barrytown, NY 12507, a not-for-profit, tax-exempt organization [501(c)(3)].

Online catalogue: www.stationhill.org
e-mail: publishers@stationhill.org

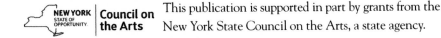 This publication is supported in part by grants from the New York State Council on the Arts, a state agency.

Cover and interior design by Susan Quasha.

Library of Congress Cataloging-in-Publication Data

Names: Hall, Nor, author. | Hall, Nor, author. End of the Iron Age.
Title: Irons in the fire / by Nor Hall.
Other titles: End of the Iron Age.
Description: Second edition. | Barrytown, NY : Station Hill of Barrytown, 2017. | Includes bibliographical references.
Identifiers: LCCN 2016046289 | ISBN 9781581771602
Subjects: LCSH: Iron industry and trade—Poetry. | Iron and steel workers—Poetry. | Iron and steel industry. | Iron and steel workers. | Myth—Psychology.
Classification: LCC PS3608.A5475 A6 2017 | DDC 811/.6—dc23
LC record available at https://lccn.loc.gov/2016046289

Manufactured in the United States of America

to
ZEUS DOLICHENUS
'born where iron arises'

in memory of
DAVID A. HALL

CONTENTS

A NOTE ON THE PROJECT

Irons in the Fire is simply one woman's love song & fear song, an epic ode to matters of a lifetime out of which iron's images extrude. It arrived unexpectedly as a result of several invitations to enter previously alien masculine territories—iron, the enemy, and war.

When Robert Cooke called from Rutgers to ask if I'd be interested in "thinking about iron," I thought, yes, in the manner of Thomas Mann who said that what was interesting was the particulars—and I knew nothing in particular about iron. At that time I was reading Anne Waldman's extraordinary poem, IOVIS, about how the archetypal masculine shows up in a woman's life. Her voice was so familiar—rising out of that place where mythologies and biographies twine, "speaking old doctrine to new form"—that it seemed suddenly necessary to follow the decades old advice of Robert Duncan at Santa Cruz to start writing poetry the way he did, imitating the style of a poet who inspires you. The poet's impetus, Cooke's invitation to address the Third International Conference on Contemporary Cast Iron Art at the Johnson Atelier in April, 1998, an invitation to Pantheatre's Myth & Theatre Festival on the Enemy in France in 1997, and my 1998 collaboration with Archipelago theater on a play called *Eulogy for a Warrior* tossed me into this swirling confluence of new material. A sluice opened, and freshly mined bits of raw information began to pour out into this hybrid piece, part-prose, part-poem.

My fascination with iron has been guided by leaders in the current revival of small-scale iron pours in North America, Great Britain and Eastern Europe –firemasters and ferrous women—whose compulsion to adore their material has bound them in essential community. I am thankful for the way they drew me to their furnace and welcomed my questions with warmth. Especially Robert Cooke, Kurt Dyrhaug, Coral Lambert, Justine Johnson, Tom Joyce, Kenneth Payne, Wayne Potratz, Tamsie Ringler and Jay Wholley. Most recently, many of us in this ragtag group of elemental iron and word practitioners met on the 2014 summer solstice at the Ped-vale Open-Air Art Museum in Latvia for the Seventh International Cast Iron Conference where I had the pleasure of telling iron's stories.

I want to thank George Quasha for imagining my original character sketch, a prose essay on mythological iron-handlers, and the praise-poem as one book. Words from the "End of the Iron Age" poem sometimes wander in and out of the expanded essay at will, appearing without attribution, exactly the way I performed them on the Atelier foundry stage, wearing red velvet gloves in an orange metallic spotlight. Everyone in Quasha's publishing circle is an artist; I'm grateful for Charles Stein's vision, Susan Quasha's ability to work under fire and the late Franz Kamin's insistence that I get rid of the dross. I also want to thank Minnesota Center for Book Arts for facilitating the first small printing of the poem bound with iron bolts and my friend Patricia Kirkpatrick for her editorial help in the new edition. My husband, Roger Hale, provided invaluable support in all ways for the initial appearance of my voice in a poem.

—Nor Hall
St.Paul, 2016

INTRODUCTION

When one of those generous ones
invites you into his fire,
go quickly!
Don't say, "But will it burn me? Will it hurt?"

—RUMI

Think of it as a day in the life of an iron pour like those popular turn of the century coffee table books "A Day in the Life of China," etc. But here the images come from descriptions of spectacular moments around hand-built furnaces fired by sculptors of contemporary art as well as from centuries of iron-handling in diverse mythologies and cultures, supplemented by my own iron-fueled travel observations in Wales, Lithuania, Morocco and China.

There is a thread of a particular day, a particular pour at a small college in northern New Jersey. Other invitational pours attended by artists from around the world at the Franconia Sculpture Garden, the University of Minnesota foundry, Rutgers University, the Johnson Atelier in Princeton, and at the historical UNESCO Ironbridge site in England weave through the text to illustrate the precise and necessary steps in every pour, from mold making and cupola construction to the final drop of the furnace "floor."

After attending my first pours I wanted to give something back to the generous ones who led me through the process. Probably the high point of my life as a word-artist happened on the occasion of the 5th Annual Cast Iron Artists Conference at Ironbridge after reading the *foo ooh ah* African bellows section from "End of the Iron Age" aloud. A few hours later, fifty of us iron workers, artists, and hangers-on crammed into the turbine house of the 18th century foundry to watch a giant steam-powered bellows pounding... when one of the men turned to me and said "It sounds just like you!"

Irons in the Fire

(A prose piece)

PRELUDE: IN THE BOEOTIAN CAFÉ

End of the Day, eighth century BCE,
Boetia Greece

In which hesiod the farmer poet, who wrote the history of the gods, coins metaliic terms for the ages and proclaims an age of iron.

Hesiod bangs his iron cup on the wooden table.

—Bring me drink! How can a man sing verse with a dry whistle?

Aidos and Nemesis, twin sisters 'Modesty' and 'Shame-Induced-by-Understandable-Anger', wrap their white aprons more tightly around their matching hips and retreat out the employee door. They walk slowly backwards together, thigh to thigh, up into the misty foothills of Mt. Helicon just as Hesiod predicted they would.

—Now, godammit, there's no help against the darkness.

Humming to himself, he taps fingers on the cup leaving smudge fossils around the greasy base. Klunk. Klunk. The distracted poet lifts the cup and drops it, lifts and drops. He does not notice the rustling of wind that starts back of his collar. It picks up a milliknot and moves aside a strand of hair covering his ear. A muse betters her aim to blow delicately into his ear through a reed pipe. She knows how to blow stories both false and true. Not the same thing as telling lies or breaking promises which are symptomatic of the Iron Age. It's more like she knows how to fabricate images out of air.

Hesiod the farmer-poet is just putting the finishing touches on his oral history of the world. He's sliding objects around on rough planks—gold nugget, silver coin, bronze medal—lining them up next to his iron cup. Other sounds flutter or amble by but nothing distracts him. He is receiving now in a direct line from Mnemosyne whose *aides memoire* ensure his getting the picture. Rags and poky implements of other farmers and sheep-tenders drift into his field of vision. He notices their mouths opening and closing at different rates and their free hands bending at wrists, rudely gesticulating, but he does not hear what they're saying.

> —Don't know why she stopped
> —Mt. Ida's flame
> —Naw
> —Sure it was... the light dimmed down
> —Vulcan's?
> —If it's not one thing it's...

Hesiod is busy coining metallic terms for the Ages. Setting them in an order pleasing to a man who could be irritatingly exact. If he'd been listening to the workers passing on the four o' clock treadmill he would have discerned the subject of their desultory conversation. "She" who stopped was the smithy's forge. Anthropomorphizing in this manner—calling the fire-stove "she" and the hammer "he" was typical worker-speak. He would be more carefully graphic in his attributions, calling the belly of the fire Bitch, the bellows Blower, the hammer Smasher and so on. Sometimes the poet tended to euphemism to distance the material from his solo table and place it more squarely in the gut of his listeners who were, after all, hungry for it.

The singer clears his throat. Benches scrape. Men spit. A goaded boy finds the jug and pours. There is audible throat-creaking among the men as minor grumbles tumble out. Dumb queries about where the women went. Across the earth-packed path, near the smoldering forge, a pair of bellows rests against a stone wall like a pair of giant wings. Hesiod readies his props. A gold nugget between his right thumb and forefinger. A sliver coin held up in his left.

—Listen. I will sum you up a tale well and swiftly!
First came the lovelier ages, Gold and Silver corresponding to
the first deathless paradise of the womb and early childhood.
Bronze followed. And men were harshly expelled into the reality
of earthly existence even before there was black Iron.

Hesiod covers the squat cup with his hand.

—Now we have nothing but labor and sorrow. Men never rest. Children age quickly and turn against their elders. No one keeps his word. Truly this is the Age of Iron. We are a foul mouthed, hardhearted race doomed to work and perish day and night.

Five pine benches groan from the weight of hopelessness. Hesiod's drone leaps toward a hymn.

—Up on the height of furrowed, windy Ida another sort of evergreen shall bear a better fruit than you laborers. For there shall mortal men get the iron that Ares loves!

The "better fruit" is iron smelted out in fires of pinewood; Ares is the god of war also known as Mars. He is the rival of Hephaistos the Vulcan, introverted fireman and ironwright, who lives deep inside the mountain. They both love iron of course, but Hephaistos is the one who arranged the ore nuts for the flame roasting to release the ore's wildness. Some ores were wild, some sour, rarely pure with the exception of the Elban. Hesiod himself had come upon traces of these ore heating circles in the rugged mountains and regarded them as signs. At such times he would pause to compose, not for willful Ares but rather for Hephaistos, the blackened anchor of home.

—Clear voiced muse, sing through me both first and last of Hephaistos, peaceful designer who, with bright-eyed Athene, teaches the glorious craft of transforming cave dwellings into gracious houses. Prosperous, hardworking, artist, ingenious tamer of fire, soot black on our behalf, we salute you and seek your favor!

FASTFORWARD

Ramapo College, late twentieth century,
early morning in the foundry yard

An invitation to speak at a cast iron foundry conference turned unexpectedly into an obsession. Hearing the muse-blown question "How would you like to think about *iron?*" tapped into my head, like the finger of a god, I said yes. Yes, not even knowing that "tapped" itself was a word-clue leading straight to the heart of the furnace. Once there had been a dream. Standing in the front hallway of a childhood home by the map drawers (plotting new directions), I asked father, "What exactly is *metallurgy...?*"

Thirty years later an answer finally dawns. It is crisp and autumnal in northern New Jersey. I've got Mircea Eliade's *The Forge and the Crucible* tucked under my imaginal belt and Wayne Potratz's *Hot Metal* guide in hand—primed for taking notes on the first full-scale iron pour I've ever attended. (A few weeks earlier I'd stopped in briefly at a pour in Minnesota but was too overwhelmed to stay for more than a 'tap'—the tapping open of the furnace that happens every twenty minutes or so at the height of a pour when the metal is melting at 2500 degrees). Sculptors in leather gear and raised plastic face shields gather like primitive aliens in the yard of the shop. The ones in chaps are foundry cowboys. There are also anachronistic looking ones in skullcaps. Like medieval workers, appearing almost menacing to a newcomer. A pile of broken radiators fills the yard by the shed. A pile of sand. Chips and donuts on a folding table. Everything is a mess. Molds are assembled on cold hard ground in an order I can't discern.

George Segal is coming to have something poured today so there is another source of excitement humming through the growing congregation.

Apparently his last mold had broken, or there hadn't been enough hot metal. I gather that major artists—certainly my friend Siah Armajani who makes bridges—tend not to pour their own iron. There's an *attitude* in the air about that choice. It has ancient roots in the art vs. craft dynamic and these people want to radically alter it. Sparks of humor fly in the foundry yard. Pick-up trucks jam the road. The pulse of activity quickens and reminds me now of a Midwestern pow-wow where ceremonial dress, food, drums and people assemble in a casual way that is a cover for the intensely absorbing trajectory of ritual.

Jane "the classicist" Harrison, talking etiology of ancient ritual, said that it was the same impulse that sent people to church and to the theatre. And, I'm thinking, to an iron pour. The ground rumbles with the import of no bull being sacrificed—at least for me. But it still seems there are priests and theatrical celebrants. One of them is walking towards me. He requests that I follow to meet the fire master who was sitting on a folding chair smoking behind the furnace. When he stands to greet me I can't believe it. He is either from central casting or all fire masters look alike. Large. Strong. A biker with a red bandana tied around his head, he drops a cigarette to shake hands. "Haven't I seen you before?" It turns out he is the same person who manned the furnace in Minnesota. Apparently there is a reserve community of iron artists on call who pack up their trucks and head out to join their friends whenever a pour is announced. It could be a turkey pour in Buffalo, a Christmas pour at Ramapo College, a thirtieth annual May pour at the University of Minnesota, a retirement pour, a summer community extravaganza pour in Herman (the town of bachelor farmers), a Halloween pour in North Carolina, a millennial pour on the coast of Scotland, a women's pour in a sculpture park, a home pour at a foundry farm. Iron artists cart their kettles across country convinced in the old alchemical tradition that this iron is no ordinary iron.

Old masters knew that the worked-on and the worker are the same. You are your own piece of art. I think these do-it-yourself cast iron artists sense the imperative of the alchemist whose lifetime task was to transmute base elements into something of value. Iron has a surface that fools you; dull, *lumpen* like Dopey the dwarf who went off to the mine everyday, as in *lumpenproletariat*. Iron lacks luster, is dense, not shiny like coal. But the *work* iron inspires is in no way dull, cannot be vague, or lack-luster energetically. On the contrary, it is quick, sure, decisive, focused, intent, calculated, skilled. Even brutal, but not mean, rather disguised like those magnetic boys in high school who wear toughness well, dress in black, smoke cigarettes burning red, their forearms like rocks. Gangs of suspect Cains—boys acquainted with the dark arts whose hot blood can be turned creative. Late bloomers. The Greeks called them Dactyls. Dactyls were priests of the great mountain goddess. Known for clashing wildly in the hills, they performed dances of secret metalworking guilds—and discovered iron smelting. Black finger digits. Bone-boys with red-hot hearts who never stray far from Mother. Iron starts out in ore form: impure, male (they thought) not virgin, already contaminated. But then it goes through a series of transformations forcing beauty out by fire.

Honk if you believe

& step into an indigo night
when only wolves could see

A heavy figure slips along the mythic path. It's the goddess Rhea pregnant. She feels her waters break and doubles over to the ground. Mother of God! Her fingers dig into earth. Iron bands contract her womb. Labor cries herald the birth of almighty Zeus. They say that wherever her fingers penetrated the dark soil a Dactyl sprung up—as many earth-spirited blood brothers as the goddess had fingers. Ten boys, born to inherit iron as their estate. Their liveliness and energy splits according to her two hands. On her right hand they are ironsmiths, the tool-graspers. On the left, they are sorcerers or shamans—the spell-casters. Always in need of each other as in the Scandinavian iron-family kinship system where devilish boys wound and their siblings, the Charm-breakers, bandage. The techniques of the artisan are connected to magic from the beginning, the magic of gifted hands blackened, bruised and bloodied by the effort of elemental birthing. Some say that Dactyls had obstetrical purpose assisting the goddess in childbirth, wielding the tools of delivery. Like the mining-dwarfs around Snow White they cluster around the woman to service her, in service of a creativity our ancestors considered divine.

SERVICING THE FURNACE

Ramapo, late morning

Standing just at the edge of the heat radius, I take in the erotic intensity of this scene. "Iron pour virgin" jokes dart through the shimmering air. There's an explanation of how to "bott" the tap hole occurring for the benefit of people who've never seen it before. Once the cupolette (a small, round, batch-melting furnace with a lid that lifts up for charging) heats the scrap iron up enough to melt the thinnest orange rivulet of molten metal, the hole at the bottom must be plugged up—quickly—with a moist mixture of mud, clay and sand clapped and molded on to the end of a metal rod like a mushroom head. This bott is aimed at the fiery hole and rammed in to stop up the flow until the fire master estimates the 300 pounds of scrap iron is melted and ready to spurt.

Servicing means being 'a slave to,' in this case, the pleasure of the furnace. Even though the furnace is usually referred to as She, "She's hot!", "She's almost ready!", the name of a furnace is not always so specifically gendered. Many have masculine names like cars called Spitfire, or a truck named Brute, (but the driver still kicks his engine over calling it "she.") This naming pattern is consistent with the traditional worker's inclination, perhaps affected in this case, perhaps not, to call the tools and machines by female handles. Iron is the commoner among noble metals and this conscious revival of its popularity among artists may loosen the *vulgar* "common" tongue that day-laborers claim and academics envy. The furnaces have colorful faces like various totems. Painted, decorated and nicknamed to reflect the soul of their makers. They announce themselves with pride as Dirty Coke Sukkah, Iron Posse, Bucksnort, Iron Circus, Shielanagig.

Naming the cupola and tools is an ancient tradition. Essentially Hephaistean. Naming bestows soul and so goes with the territory of the ultimate craftsman who, among the Greek gods, was such an excellent artist that he "profoundly confused nature and art." Any object crafted by his hand, from iron anvil to golden bracelet, could move and breathe. Like the famous shield Hephaistos made for Achilles undulating with running rivers, vines and leaping animals. Why not name such a shield? Or your furnace for that matter, because it is alive. Wherever work is so elementally transformative, worker's implements are ensouled. It's a wise move to have a relationship with objects that could kill you. Jealousy, contentment, withdrawal, ecstasy, rage. Strong human emotions thrive in the circle of the blast furnace. With regard to jealousy for example, the furnace tolerates no distraction. The focus of the fire-tender's energy must be on the needs of the furnace. He (or she) must be as alert as a lover to the level of the flame, the timing for the charge, the size of the openings, whether or not "she" is content as in the stories of a Mr. Zippler's furnace that wouldn't perform for anyone else. Or sister cupolas that had to be separated.

In parts of Africa, iron attendants were required to be celibate. All available energy goes into the furnace the way all available thought-waves go into fanning obsessive love. Being an accomplished fire master requires a nighttime of preparation (under the right phase of the moon) with extraordinary attention to detail, extreme care for the body of the furnace, tenderness of technique, focusing, finding the right rhythm for blasting and breathing. Bamanan blacksmiths in Mali still make necklaces out of miniature iron tongs for expectant mothers. A blacksmith's fearlessness in handling glowing metal is like a woman's courage during her body's "hot ordeal." Ritual celibacy was grounded in devotion for metallurgical artists, the iron-smelting priests of Cybele, the dwarfish masters of initiation, and the warrior Cuchulain of Irish epic known as the 'Hound of the Forge.' Passion draws women close to the fires of all of these gods, but the women who venture forward don't stay for long. Aphrodite is drawn to Hephaistos like an iron magnet—to his skill, his magical hands—but his forge is like another woman. So she leaves for the love of a different fiery god who is not forge-bound. When they are in the throes of melting metal the iron gods are not free to follow the dictates of any other passion or to follow the enticements of beauty apart from the deepest one issued from within the material itself. Iron's fire requires absolute fidelity.

Listen *homo faber*,

there is always a woman in the fire

Hesiod tells a story about how "the famous limping god" Hephaistos took the elements of earth and water and fully figured out the first woman *in the fire*. Like anything he ever touched his sculpture came alive and he called her Pandora. Another time he fashioned silent virgin robots that swiveled golden-hipped around his forge, but Pandora "the giver of gifts" was graced with a seductive, melodious voice. Strange pictures of her as a great female head rising up out of the ground show her in profile flanked by swarthy men wielding hammers and pick-axes. Godly gadabouts. (A gad is a miner's tool for chipping rock). Pandora was being mined, or else hammered into shape on the anvil of earth. Her seductiveness according to Hesiod, who is generally suspicious, lends the iron god's woman a double nature that is inherent to iron.

Iron is famously duplicitous. It bursts upon the world riding a great wave of usefulness. But household objects, utilitarian devices, articles of adornment, utensils for cooking and farm implements all issue from the same sweltering belly that bears weapons of torture and destruction. "Doubly victorious!" is the cry of the Iron Age: creating civilization on the one hand and destroying it on the other. Even Pandora's "box" releases a host of ills along with an embryo of hope. Every forge and furnace has its firebox functioning like a necessary womb for the worker. The items that emerge, to continue the litany of iron, are "as essential in warfare as in the welfare of earth's people"; "to be feared and to be adored"; "war's vehicle and yet the central implement in the beneficent spread of agriculture." If you pursue these duplicitous roots of things all-good and evil, the pursuit soon gives way to multiplicity. There is a tremendously rich story contained in the memory of iron. Its gifts, like Pandora's simplified, hardly break down according to the dual production line of plows and swords, because iron ore comes naturally without bias into the lap of men in the Iron Age who melt or mold it into shape. And they, the shapers, are not only martial *or* pacifist in intent. Sometimes they are craftsmen of the hearth, passionate lovers of matter's form—artists who adorn and caress their material.

Iron men and ferrous women get caught red-handed in the service of art. They say there's a wild man in Texas who dares slap the stream barehanded, the way you pass a finger through candle flame. To do iron you have to place yourself within fire's range to learn its ways. Whet your tongue on its lexicon of heat. Expose your flesh to iron's sizzling-tipped shafts of eros. Eros is going where you're driven but not allowed to go. Part of the excitement in ironwork is disobedience, being drawn to secret fires. The first thing we ever learn about fire is not to touch it. Early prohibition leads to an early desire to disobey. "Hot!" Even though the work is surrounded with rules meant to protect, collective ardor repeatedly melts the blocked mass into molten, flowing streams remarkably like love when blocked desire is heated to the melting point.

ACCIDENTS HAPPEN

Ramapo, mid day

An artist in full leather gear & steel-toed boots is leaping over the row
of molds and tearing at his left sock. Sock, boot and pants all come off in
a matter of seconds. His alarm spreads to the onlookers, some of whom
dash for cold water, but the team carrying the neon ladle can not and
does not waver in their task. Inching cautiously down the mold row they
pour their precious molten cargo into the black holes that gape like wide-
mouthed birds of hell. Some of these molds have styrofoam linings and
smoke horribly. This pour is outside and the toxic waste spirals up into the
atmosphere where Hephaistos is the only god I can imagine being pleased
to receive this smoky mortal offering: he whose lungs were coated black
like bellows.

—Here, put these on.

I am being dressed for my turn at the presently botted-up red-hot hole
and am about to get my first lesson in the kinesthetic origin of archetypal
imagery. I think these duds are like my name—they provide gender-cover.
Leather aprons clip around back and large gloves protect hands of any size.
Apparently there are jokes about everything. The men who wear chaps
over their jeans seem dangerously exposed in front—like they might want
an asbestos codpiece—but they make cracks about covering their asses
(which are not covered). These clowns, serious as they are, descend in a
direct line from German ironworkers in the eighteenth century who wore
multi-purpose *arschleders*, literally arse-leathers. Worn backwards, they
were useful for sliding down mine shafts. Turned to the front, the leathers
became protective aprons at the forge. Before dressing to go to work the

wearer performed a magical rite of jumping over the *arschleder* for courage; like a prayer, his leap (*ledersprung*) signified willingness to jump into and back out of the world of danger. It's curious that workers also wore this same garment, turned backwards like formal "tails," for ceremony. There must be an original stone-carved lithograph somewhere of dwarfs dressed-up in traditional miner's garb on their way to Snow White's wedding. Clearly this intricate wardrobing process is initiatory, not only for me, but, for anyone who wants to get close to the mystery.

The headgear fits like a helmet with a clear shield that flips down to cover my glasses. Leather boots are the best I could do—not steel-toed, but they won't burn easily. I've heard stories of fire immunity from many places, like the kahunas who can walk across incandescent lava, or the three biblical survivors thrown into a furnace so hot it burned up the guard without singeing a hair on their heads. My faith in my ability to handle this approach to the furnace is lamentably far from that steady state. A friend (the artist who originally asked me to think about iron) comes up behind me and says he'll be right there. I know I can trust him. The team is buoyed by mutual tenderness for their task. Someone told a horror story about an iron master who didn't like his guys wearing earrings; how he bullied them with the threat of holding an ear to the cupola. But there's no sign of sadism here and no excuse for me not to step forward to pick up my end of the pole attached to the ladle bucket. The pole on the other side extends a few feet from the bucket and forks in order to permit two team members to carry and tip it out together. My responsibility, with flexed knees and fierce grip, is to keep my end level so that the brilliant, burning liquid won't slop over the sides before we reach the mold.

> set-apart by physical defect & oddities of accident
> the metal worker limps from the burning cave

coming down from the hills

>   his breath is fire
>   his glance a blaze
>   condensed
>   not luminous
>   or heavenly
>
>   looking at him
>   I stare into a furnace

Accidents are a big part of the lore around melting metal. Two magical smoke-covered shrines affixed to the wall between the furnace and the ladle mark a highly dangerous intersection at the university foundry in Minnesota. Our Lady of the Cupola raises her right hand index finger in a serene gesture indicating a plastic lizard on top of her halo. Perhaps this creature is a reference to the rejuvenating salamander of the alchemists that would change color and state when thrown into the fire. The Lady is draped with soiled bandana, rosary beads, crow's feather, a scroll, Guatemalan bracelets, a brass bell, an interstate Detroit diesel cap, and a St. Odilia holy card: all protective objects. The other shrine looks Japanese. Literally charming. It's covered with crescent moon amulets, temple charms, a small silver disco ball, plastic fish, play money, a dangling Day of the Dead skeleton, kitty cat collar, bull dog charm, Japanese rice candy, cigarettes, dried four leaf clover, incense and an iron poppy. This last item gives me pause. A poppy is the *narke* flower (as in narcotic) of the Underworld and belongs to the realm most feared by iron miners. Death guards its treasures and delivers them up only to those who keep a foot in both worlds. Or keep a root in the depths like that of the red flower. When made out of iron and placed in the shrine this death-inducing poppy becomes a tribute to another of the Underworld gods, Ogun, whose bone-vibrating message - *stay alert!* - gets drummed daily into his people.

Fire alerts the imagination to potential danger. In contemporary Yoruba culture foundrymen, railroad workers, steel cutters, cab drivers, key & baton-carrying night watchmen—anyone coming in contact with fire-born iron—still say daily prayers to Ogun for protection from accidents. A deep-rooted wariness about this metal is reflected in the assignment of a marginal place to the metal worker who has to handle something so loaded. Because iron is an abnormally potent and supernaturally endowed element, Ogun, who *is* iron, is regarded with tremendous ambivalence. He causes disasters and protects from disaster at the same time. His sub-Saharan street god character is marked by the same shifting and uneasy nature that marks iron men everywhere.

There is a story about how Ogun functions as protector and destroyer of his own village. One day he was leaving his people (although he was their leader, Ogun was ordinarily a recluse who preferred living beyond the reach of civilization). He attached himself to a rope and went down into a deep hole in the ground and told the people that if they ever needed him all they had to do was pull on the cord. Time went by. They hadn't heard from Ogun in a long while which made one of the villagers increasingly anxious so, one day, he took it upon himself to test the rope to see if Ogun was really there. He gave the rope a slight pull and in an instant Ogun blasted out of the hole in the ground, whirling in a fire-rage, slashing and burning destroying everything in sight. Thinking that his full powers were needed, he released a whirlwind of ultimate destruction and obliterated every man, woman and child in sight—not one of them an "enemy".

The rope puller had been an indiscriminate iron handler. Iron on a leash signals times of quiet productivity and artful calm for the village. *Un*leashed it means bloodshed, destruction, cruel and indiscriminate change. Iron itself is blind but full of potential like the ore-god hidden in the shaft. The gut deep ambivalence in the god's nature is informed by this capacity of iron to explode into flying hot particles like a weapon in inexperienced hands. Or it can be directed—worked or channeled by the wise-handler into new forms that provide stability to protect the patterns of everyday life in human community.

Not only is Ogun *both* leader and recluse, he is a benefactor and pariah, vengeful and beneficent, brave and opportunistic—his nature is essentially connected to technology, material innovation, and cultural change. Most Yoruba cults concentrate on the unknown, inexplicable forces of nature but Ogun's expertise is different. He specializes in the human realm of regulating power unleashed by men. Industrial strength gains a momentum of its own that becomes quickly dangerous. Consequently, the code of Ogun's current warriors, (i.e. metal workers, mechanics, sculptors, & engineers) says watch out for the accidental. Take that which potentially disrupts and monitor it, even better, *transform* it. Put it to the heat, pound the hell out of it, melt it down and reshape its nature.

Any two iron objects placed with intention—two simple nails, or a gun and a crowbar, tongs or an iron poppy—become an altar generating sanctuary, a neutral zone or safe-place to pause in recognition of the dangerous divinity of iron. In New York city once I stepped over a curb and saw two nails crossed on a silver foil gum wrapper lying in the street. Iron bars bear the weight of truth in African courtrooms where iron is sworn on instead of a Bible. Any foundry gives sanctuary, all forges are altars.

—"You have to be cool to handle Ogun."

In Los Angeles where there are signs of the god present in spirit-shops that handle the accouterments of his cult, it was only Ogun's shop that remained standing in a block decimated by riots in 1992. A priest who was in the shop at the time described the insurrection as *an Ogun event.* Things got too hot and Ogun needed cooling down. While store fronts were exploding, he washed the altar with water from a gourd, reminiscent of the way his grandfather washed the killing from the face of a deranged hunter or murderer by pouring the cooling water from the village blacksmith's forge over the man's face three times a day for seven days to take the rage out of him. Ogun is feared, but necessary in dangerous times. When everything is blocked you want someone forceful to unleash the risky power necessary for breakthrough. That is why they say, in this religion of iron, that you are a child until you become a fire master capable of holding Ogun in your hand.

CHILD'S PLAY

Twenty minutes and counting down. While I dress in the second team's outfit, the first team completes the charge process. Once it was determined that the entire bed of coke was burning, the fire master blasted the firebox through the bottom tap hole for five minutes then adjusted the bed height before signaling the furnace sibyl. She balances on a tripod stool. He lifts the lid and adjusts the coke height. Then she takes buckets passed by brigade, hand over hand, from the scrap radiator pile and empties them into the gullet of the cupolette. Like the head of the serpent at Chitzenitsa at the moment of the equinox illumination, all the energy seems to be passing down the line through to her face and upper body as she stands over the heat of the fire. The molten millstone maw slams shut. I am permitted to get close enough to the wind box to peer inside the hole when liquid iron starts to drop. These little muse-windows called *tuyeres* create an opening from the air source to the interior of the furnace just like the reed pipes that blew inspiration into the head of the poet.

The first Chinese furnaces had many breath-pipes funneled into the body of the furnace. These were followed historically by air propulsion mechanisms: foot-powered bellows, water wheels, and now machines that roar like industrial vacuums in reverse. One of the foundry men used an old Chrysler slant-six car engine to blast his fire. Another tries diesel fuel sending more black smoke up to choke the blue sky. He is the same innovator who worked under the pressure of hundreds of eyes to win the Smallest Cupola Contest at the conference by making a miniature, hand-sized blast furnace. He melted enough iron to pour an actual, knuckle-sized piece of art in under twenty minutes.

I regret not asking that foundry man what he was doing when he was nine years old. That age seems to be an extraordinarily formative time in the life of gods and mortals. Fortunate souls who have periods of required separation from home in order to undergo an initiation process (where their mettle gets cast) find themselves swept into a whirlwind like Dorothy leaving Kansas at about that age. Just on the brink of major gender assertion when there is still a little bit of time to experiment freely without the sexual pressure to fulfill a certain role. Gods used to protect this vulnerable time for girls and boys in order to let them play with toys of identity. For example Athena, goddess of wisdom and also war, in her most archaic form was called Goddess of the Coal Pan. Like every woman rampant to dress like a man to get near fire, she was born in full battle gear out of the head of her father, Zeus, with the dactylic aid of an iron hammer. Even though her character seemed fully forged, she was handed over to a foundry in North Africa to be raised by a Cyclops.

Cyclops are cave dwelling forge-giants who live at the foot of volcanoes alongside tempering rivers. Savage appetites and only one eye each. Called Flash, Thunderer, Striker and Firestone, their one-eye signifies singleness of purpose. As father-substitutes they are blind to any interest other than their own gigantic expertise, fostering only a fascination with the fire and its products. I think of the one-eyed craters burning like the sun on top of the pyramid on our dollar bills. That unwavering gleam a miner's lamp, focusing, getting to the point, wanting only its own climax and shutting out all intrusion.

The girl Athena forged her own spear and then challenged a playmate, Pallas, a natural daughter of the cyclopean smith Brontes, to a game that turned deadly. Living at the base of the founder's fire, the goddess had learned her lessons well. Athena may not have known her own strength and, unable to avert her perfect aim, killed Pallas. Utterly distraught after accidentally killing her foundry sister, she set up a shrine for Pallas and hung her sacred, protective goatskin shield on it. Almost like furnace chaps. Any foundry implement in her hands—solid hammer, slender spear—would unfailingly hit its mark. A particular shadow of the ironworker lurks behind this singleness of aim that illuminates exactly what it shines its light on. The other side of *focus* is limited vision. One-eyed vision allows no openings for ambiguity, tolerates no accidents, and is blind to any other way of proceeding. A mind made up is iron clad.

Hephaistos was another serious child born to the gods and sent off to be raised by Libyan smiths. Known as "heaven's reject," the first thing you notice about images of him is his density and physical distortion. He is ugly, compact, swarthy, and bent out of shape. Unlike the beautiful Apollo who is born successful and who represents the radiant accomplished perfection of the human spirit, Hephaistos carries all the dark contents of bad relationship. He was born to feuding parents, at a time in pre-history when the feminine principle wanted acknowledgement for the capacity to create independently. Zeus had just given birth to Athena by himself so why shouldn't the goddess Hera try the same thing? The goddess gave birth in revenge and was delivered of an outrageously odd, dwarfish, smoldering future craftsman—not an elegant work of art. So she threw him furiously to the earth. He fell for a day to the island of Lemnos, lungs-smashed, barely a breath in the bellows. Some say she was a more generous mother and took him to Kedalion (the old Crab or Phallic One), a primal forge master who taught him to excel in mastery of fire. Still another thread of the story says he was raised by sea nymphs who caught him in their lovely, receptive arms when he fell from heaven. Out of gratitude for their ministrations, the outcast god spent his earliest years hunched over a child-sized forge. While his sister Athena was hammering iron spears and dancing around coal pans in North Africa, he was fashioning marvelous jewelry, delicate belt-buckles, and floral necklaces for women he loved.

Suddenly everything goes silent. All eyes focus on the tap hole. Expectation makes a quiet space around the hand of the man who picks the bott. A rush of liquid metal gushes from the tap hole. The blazing orange arc is greeted with ecstatic cries, the very shouts Hera, alas, longed to hear aeons ago from the mouths of exuberant dwarf midwives:

—It's a big one!
—A rooster tail!
—Sweet!
—Good looking!

Now I am pressed into service. I have never been so close to terrifying heat. Gray black gunk is skimmed off the top of the bubbling liquid. The molten neon brew bursts with golden tapioca bubbles. It's an active smoking volcano that I bend to pick up and carry. Rising from crouched position with the ladle of liquid fire between me and the other carrier I am startled by a Hephaistian epiphany. We walk in hunched tandem backwards and sideways around the molds that wait open-mouthed for their fix. This awkward crab-like pattern of movement is dictated by the necessity of the work and is exactly how the master smith moved. He *scuttled* from side to side, or backwards with a peculiar rolling gait, panting as he went. His nicknames—Panter, Puff-Monster, Blast-breather—are all sounds easy to identify in this moment of exertion. This way of moving requires sure instinct and vigilance. It is indirect, sometimes circumambulatory, going in circles and sometimes tacking, switching from one approach to another to arrive at a specific goal. I've caught the ecstasy of the pour-trance in this moment but am also extremely glad to be spotted because my arms, flexed to tip the one hundred pound ladle, are giving out.

Sometimes Hephaistos' peculiar movement is attributed to his being chained to the forge. His moves in relation to his work are very similar to a scuttle of labor on life's problems that anyone can recognize, an eternity of reaching sideways for the tongs, starting back from the flame, holding and hammering and thrusting and quenching, rotating in place around a core issue without moving very far. One of the psyche's gestures similar to the dream where you get stuck with your legs feeling heavier and heavier. As if they are solidifying into iron. No matter how hard you try to run you are rooted to the spot so that the thing that is trying to get you will get you. This process of solidification or fixation fits Hephaistos whose bottom half is in league with the underworld. The underworld Darkers, the "things that are trying to get you", cripple the one who wants to be up and running smoothly in the dayworld and instead pull it down and down into the workshop of Hephaistos. His unmatched ability as a matured artisan is that he can work his way out of the shadows by ingenious invention, casting new images out of life scraps, character distortions, and discards. Ultimately the beauty of his work is in the twist—that he has a foot in both worlds: the first piece he ever made was a pair of precious metal prosthetic legs to facilitate the adjustment of his own stance. His myth suggests that the god-given urge to make something out of nothing is buried at the base of our psyches. As if the urge dwells in an internal volcano. *Homo faber*, man the maker, does not create or conceive in this instance, but rather shapes and changes existing materials, actively constructing, fitting together, molding into shape. Hephaistos the earthly Maker (as opposed to heavenly Maker) works underground with what has been given, like Thor his gigantic Nordic counterpart, reaching beneath earth's crust to knead molten magma with bare hands.

In conversation with my father after the iron pour weekend I note that the foundry professors remind me of my deceased brother who did metal. He was a slave to fire like all the other boys his age doing chemistry experiments in Vulcan's basement. Later he took up welding in the garage, fabricating precious jewelry in the studio and fashioning prosthetic devices, a limb sculptor in the tradition of the strange blacksmith god. He really was Hephaistean.

My father and I think quietly for a moment. Then he speaks to deliver an ancestral gift out of the blue, but fired directly from the fantasy world of my great aunts unknown to me.

—The Cory-Lyman family had a foundry in Jersey City near the Delaware & Hudson canal, on the bay in the 1850's, maybe a little later. They built it on the bay because of a lock system on the canal. For shipping coal. Uzal Cory owned it. He refined gold and silver at his company in New York and made furnaces at the foundry in New Jersey. His nieces, the Henry Lyman girls Clementine and Virginia, used to play in the back yard making clay furnaces, firing them with twigs.

POTENT ARTICULATOR

Ramapo, mid afternoon

Everyone has an iron-handling ancestor in the family. Prior to the spread of the late Judeo-Christian map over the imagination of the West, which sucked divinity up exclusively to heaven, the earth and the underworld were lively places, ensouled and rich with meaning. Iron belonged to the underworld, to Hades. Even when it was meteoric and sent zinging down from the sky in the form of Zeus' lightning bolt, it was given a throne beneath earth's surface. David Smith, talking about why he used to collect scrap iron, said:

—Before I knew what art was I was an ironmonger. The iron element I hold in high respect. I consider it eidetic in property.

Eidetic means that it contains images. Iron itself retains visual images in its memory. Each piece of crafted iron has a journey as long as Cain's, the great grandfather of iron working who began his journey in a hard-hearted rage that fed on itself for centuries. After murdering his brother—the Able farmer—he passed through rage, survived God's kicking him out of Eden and traveled through the endlessly arid terrain of emotional isolation. On the far side of the Land of Nod he found his tongue again in a new community. Even though the metal itself is inarticulate, Old Testament scripture tells us that Cain eventually had three children: the brothers Iron-man, Word-sparker and Leather-handler. Three brothers emerged from the same womb to tend fire, poetry and sheep. All solitary wanderers who pursue their craft in proximity. Their fraternity is still evident in iron-pour pastures like this one where I hear a voice coming from the other side of the furnace. An iron elder shouts out Robert Frost's apocryphal poem.

Some say the world will end in fire
some say in ice
from what I've tasted of desire
I hold with those who favor fire!

Iron attracts poetry. It needs the mediation of the poet because it is uncivilized. Its potency is so dangerous that it roars for containment, like the bursting rage of Cain. Either the containment of words, or a womb-like animal container for example, made of leather. An African Mande smith whose intensive training is based on the acquisition of knowledge about three things, *gundow* (trade secrets of iron work) *jiridon* (the science of trees that provide fuel) and *daliluw* (constellations of materials and procedures that allow people to accomplish things), is also always a leather worker who makes small pouches for holding iron talismans. He is called the "potent articulator" because his arduous training in the handling of spiritual forces translates into messages pounded into iron for his clients.

Last year in a sticky packed Berber souk outside of Marrakech, I stopped to watch a blacksmith sitting under a makeshift tent with a low anvil and circle of glowing coals between his scarred legs. (He sat on a stack of hides instead of wearing the protective leathers). Five different sizes of rods, and tongs radiated out of the hot circle like black spokes. When he picked up his hammer he grunted at a younger man in the shadows who swung around sideways, pivoting on his arm like a crab, into the front of the tent, squatting by the firestone and raising a hammer with both hands. Then they began an extraordinary conversation like a piece of performance art. *Kling-klang-kling...* It started with each man playing the perfect rhythmic counterpart to the other and grew in audible color and complexity. The elder held the glowing piece of iron on the anvil stone with tongs in his left hand and hammered with his right. Lifting and lowering their hammers to ring down on hot iron, they added an airy descant of sound issuing from their bellies. Surely a kind of poetry. The only thing missing was the group of women described in *The Mande Blacksmith* sitting opposite, pounding grain in pestles held between their knees. Each thud accompanying the contrapuntal klang of the forge and accented by praise-words for food and metal.

—Are they revered?

Latif, our gentle guide, restrained himself in answering. He gave a gruff, one word, educated dismissal. So this must be a place, I gathered, where iron's lineage was dethroned either by its suspicious shamanic associations or by its wandering history. Nomads used iron more for weaponry, starting with the hunter's spear that kills, whereas settled agricultural communities used it for hoes and ploughs to make seedstones blossom into fruit. These associations stuck according to Eliade. Iron and ironworkers were set-apart for being powerful in either case. But the blood-spill culture's blacksmiths were left outside the gate to become low-level technicians (and black magicians) while the farmer's blacksmiths were revered for their priestly ability to bless life and make it flourish. Opposing priesthoods-of-iron spilled their identical white-hot gold into history's trough for so long that this theoretical split doesn't truly hold—but something archaic was operating in this Moroccan standoff. Later, Latif mentioned the significant presence of iron in the Koran.

Practitioners of iron art seem often to be men of few words. Of course this is a stereotype, but stereotypes have tendrils sunk into the authentic soil of archetypal imagery so they can carry precise truths. When a certain kind of iron man does get words, he seems to be getting whatever he has to sing or say from iron itself. In old Austria this was explained by the figure of the *Berggeist*—the spirit of the mountain that lived in iron mines and competed in a typical way with the "spirits" a man could get in a tavern. Joseph was one such man who would always sing over his drink after the days iron work was done. But then he started singing down below while hewing rock for ore. Soon his pile of iron ore grew so large that the overseers were astonished. They congratulated him by paying him and then moved him to successively more difficult veins. He sang loudly those nights as he quaffed the tavern's spirits but one day his task appeared so huge that it sobered him to a silent stare. Suddenly a tiny man in black garb appeared standing on the rock ledge and commanded Joseph to sing. When Joseph asked why, the gnome said it lifted his spirits and that the more Joseph sang the more he would do the work of extracting iron. Joseph sang and sang and sang in the mines and the gnome made his pile grow into a mountain. His cohorts became jealous and eventually plied the resistant miner with enough drink to make him spill his secret source. Then jealousy worked its deadly games. Joseph was killed by the gnome in a ghastly mining accident (on record in Rudolstadt, 1678), his piles of iron gone. No more song. And eventually his so-called friends perished by suspicious accident in the very same hole.

A dead singer, or poet, is an *impotent articulator*. While alive, both their liveliness and their livelihood come from an edgy place of danger. Anyone who works with iron has to be constantly aware of disaster and develop an extra-sensory field of awareness around themselves that is grounded, absolutely, in the body. Every apperceptive particle in the artist's cellular make-up has to be on alert. Especially around the fire, but not only then. His hands (or hers) have to be working with dangerous tools and chemicals and extraordinarily heavy objects in places where the footing is insecure and it's impossible to see. The author of the first *Pirotechnia*, the sixteenth century fire-technician and poet Biringuccio, noted the risky ensnarement of metal:

This art holds the mind of the artificer in suspense and fear and keeps his spirit disturbed and almost continually anxious. For this reason they are called fanatics and are often unable to leave the place of work despite the discomforts that must be sustained. Unnatural heats, unbearable wet colds, accidents, dirt and danger... these labors are endured with pleasure and the outcome awaited with such desire that the artificer is ensnared.

Every iron artist has their own story of being entranced by the material and unable to leave. A pour is only the climax of an intense process that reaches back into the hinterland of the imagination the way the source of the ore itself reaches endlessly deep within the earth. When Novalis, the mining engineer & poet of minerals, went exploring iron mines in the 1800's he saw stars in the depths "glittering as if in heavenly constellation". He thought of iron miners as astrologers in reverse, seeking, as he was, the distant hidden source for the heat that fueled his life. For Novalis that was poetry.

Robert Duncan, the twentieth century poet I mentioned earlier, used to describe being unable to leave a poem the way the artificer of iron was unable to leave his place of work. As a child he had been fascinated by the visual play of tempering metal. How red metal would glow white and be plunged into a water bucket set there "to catch a star." This early experience of the *tremendum* registered in his liquid reading voice that sometimes flowed, sometimes grew grave & steely. He identified with the Dactyls who knew how to trace the mother lode, mine it for material, and introduce it to the refining fire. About writing he said, " Being in a temper is part of my voice in a poem". He even wore a black swirling cape with a dactyl-like hood to pull up against the California fog. It made him look gnarly and dwarfish, stomping out the pace of a poem as he walked—eyes fixed, ears smoking.

Duncan was "one crazy Orisha" as one poet says of another. In Ogun's territory that meant spirit-spokesperson. The one possessed by divinity's power sang the *ijala* chants to invoke the terrifying energy. Bold fire-straddlers, crazy with machetes, men and women both called—in precise poetic form—to the Owner of All Iron to come fast. To work his contradictory miracles. Staunch blood, fill a woman, slice a road through the forest, cut the animal's throat, make peace, or crown a king as in a Rilke poem where the young warrior is given a drink from an iron headpiece; is it wine, he wants to know, or blood?

Pow! pow! pow! sounds like *pa pa pa*, kill kill kill in Ogun's chant. If sound can be eidetic too, then memory of iron's explosive nature is expressed in *p*'s and *k*'s constantly filling adherent's mouths (speaking their *muthos*, myth). *Ppuh ppuh* pants Hephaistos at the foundry as he forges fury into links of an invisible net to catch his aphroditic wife *in flagrante*. Kuh kuh is the sound of any kids gun. Ogun *is* gun, iron chain (klank), knife. *Keh ge keh ge keh ge keh ge* is the sound of a head rolling in the wake of his mad blade. Sounds of violence carry the injunctive prayers that urge petition, "Please, Lord (of Iron) keep us out of your necessary death path."

> On the days Ogun is angered,
> there is always death in the world.
> The world is full of dead people going to heaven.
> The eyelashes are full of water.
> Tears stream down the face.
>
> Ogun let me not see the red of your eye.
> Ogun is a crazy *orisha* who still asks questions after 780 years!
> Whether I can reply, or whether I can not reply,
> Ogun please don't ask me anything.

It is said that the iron god was wounded and his wound forced him to wander from town to town all over the country asking questions of the people: What does iron want of you? How will you handle it? The only way for him to heal his immortal wound was to be an itinerant wordsmith. He put the garment of skillful song on his glowing back and traveled in black smoke with a dog running alongside. Moving by enchantment, he taught the exact *ijala* patterns that could carry the weight of his presence. Preciseness of technical form goes hand in hand with the shaman's healing ecstasy. Ritual song, poetry and movement require careful technique, attention to detail, following rules, sequential steps. When Ogun de Fer rides the body of his carrier in a vodun ceremony it will always be the same dance to a practiced eye. Spontaneous trance dancing looks wild and abandoned but adheres to archetypal pattern. And so it is with the firing of this furnace. The ecstatic epiphany of art is only arrived at by an exact process critically timed. If you visit a foundry during a pour and watch the process at a slight distance without the distractions of sound and smell—it looks like a dance choreographed by the most potent iron-handler present who seems to hold center stage and run the periphery simultaneously.

SAVAGE & SOLITARY BEAST

Ramapo, later afternoon

Back in place behind the rangy phalanx of molds, I watch the furnace team synchronize their moves for the third charge of the day. The mold captain wears a black t-shirt with a flaming red-eyed skull on the back. Another man's shirt reads *Illuminati*. This pour's skimmer and tippers—the ones who will be closest to the burst of liquid fire—pass the buckets of pig iron again to feed the Mouth that's open and glowing like Satan's maw. It's burning at such an extraordinary temperature that the asbestos glove of the tamper catches on fire. Smoke partially obscures the cupolas shimmering deadly neon grin. Even on this small scale it is possible to imagine the ominous instruction of a grandmother in Birmingham, Alabama who took a child to see the awesome ridge of hulking furnaces belching smoke, lit up like massive fiery dungeons, throwing liquid sparks of lava onto the black breast of night. "Hell," she told her, "watch out, this is what it's like."

Segal's sculpture is done. Fortunately there was enough iron this time to fill every crevasse of the mold. The professor whom I'd identified as Priest of the Pour takes a break and crosses over to the observers' side where I am told he is the one who held the legendary Christmas Day pour. *Ignis Divinus!* Another unlikely source of violent imagery from the furnace of European folklore renders Jesus Christ (or St. Nicholas, hence Christmas) into a fire-god, *Ignite-the-Divine*. Master of Masters. He hung his shield over a forge and after magically shoeing the blacksmith's horse, took the old man's just-dead wife and threw her onto the fire. Using the anvil of the smith he pounded her back into shape whereupon she rose up breathing and young with blossoms of fire in her cheeks. Others tried to imitate his feat with disastrous results. You had to *be* the sacred fire handler to accomplish it.

St. Nick belongs in the chimney. Like Hephaistos who fashioned Pandora, he brings dolls to life as a sign of the rejuvenating power of heat, fire and light. The sacred fire handlers gift mortals with Light at the year's darkest point. Cinderella belongs in this folkloric corner too—guarding the dying coals of the fire with meager hope and ample fantasy. *Cinder* (burnt wood that still emits light but no flame) *ella* (light's message) is kin to the Russian Vasilissa, the girl with a protective doll in her pocket, who is sent by her three wretched sisters to Baba Yaga in order to get fire for their fizzling hearth. She brings it back at night in a flaming skull on a stick. Unearthly fire curls from its eyes and nose and ears, terrifying to the uninitiated but animating to the cold hearth. It's a charge to those who can handle it.

In the sixteenth century there was a man with an encyclopedic appreciation of metal's spiritual requirements. Johannes Mathesius, who sat at Martin Luther's dinner table to discuss his metallic visions, used to dress in ironworkers garb to speak to his flock of *Bergmann*—mountain men whose lives revolved around digging ore and firing furnaces. Unfortunately his Sixteen Mountain Sermons on Metal (an intentional pun on Sermons on the Mount) have never been translated. Sermon number Eight was written in 1562: *On Iron, Steel and the Columns of Daniel*. Pastor Mathesius clearly loved his element. From what I can tell, his intention was like Hesiod's, to honor the name and nature of iron "without which no house on earth could exist." He's a namer and a praiser speaking directly to the "amazing and lovely hearts" of the mountain people who dwell in the craft of iron with a kind of wisdom he attributed to Daniel. Daniel was the biblical interpreter for King Nebuchadnezzar's dream about the towering statue who had the sun for a head, calves of iron, and, alas, feet of clay (i.e. a mountain). Mathesius knows his scriptural references (Daniel

35

2.31-46, Job 6, Psalms 18, Matthew 6.19, Deuteronomy 34.24) but he also knows his technical data and fills fifty pages with intricate detail about tools of extraction, gorgeous metaphor about iron's depth & intractability and intriguing references to the lives of the men whose bodies sweat blood for iron's sake and for the sake of refining their souls in the fire of the heavenly Mountain King. A lexicon of his terms has been published (also in German) with hundreds of metal related entries introduced by an acknowledgement that *the stones are our silent teachers*.

The traditional price of working with iron is marginalization—an awkward word meaning that you live on everyone else's edge. Iron masters are at home with what other people consider unmanageable, *darke & foule*. Mathesius' ironworkers lived on the side of the mountain "where no ray of sun ever shone." Imagination ascribes darkness to the dwelling place of those whose grueling work it is to supply the forge and foundry. Appreciation for their crucial labor is underscored by fear and distaste and only voiced with enthusiasm at a distance as in the wary Mande furnace chant: "*Ah savage and solitary beast, we cannot finish praising you!*" Those who represent handlers of iron on a cosmic scale (Greek, African, Japanese, Siberian, Celtic) all radiate this grotesque glory of an isolated divine Beast. No one really wants to get too close.

A description of the Irish hero Cuchulain (Kuh *hool* un) sounds precisely like a blast furnace with regard to his grotesque transformation. His name means Hound of the Smith because he killed the smith's guard-dog when he was nine years old and was then hired on as forge guardian in place of the dog. In order to become the greatest warrior who ever lived, he had to pass through an apprenticeship by the fire. Later, it turns out that he *becomes* the iron smelter—all roaring, fire-breathing torso in battle where his primary feat was a violent bodily distortion called a "warp-spasm" that turned him into a fighting machine so hot that metal melted in his throat:

The spasm made him into a monstrous thing—his face and features became a red bowl... his mouth weirdly distorted: his cheeks peeled back from his jaws until the gullet appeared... his lower jaw struck the upper a lion-killing blow and the fiery flakes large as a ram's fleece reached his mouth from his throat.... Malignant mists and spurts of fire—the torches of the Badb—flickered red in the vaporous cloud that rose boiling above his furious head.

The next morning Cuchulain would be returned to his manly form and come out to display himself to the Queen because he knew his horrible distortion didn't do his beauty justice. Then he would appear radiant, handsome & glowing (subdued *furor*) in all the colors associated with the splendor of fire and iron—even his hair was described as flowing in ferrous strands of crimson, gold, and rust. Ogun went through a similar physical transformation. Iron men (and women) are masters of extremes. "When working he has little care for his appearance, is inarticulate, and has trouble communicating with people. He prefers strong drink and smells of blood and sweat. When at rest he is bathed in an aromatic herbal concoction, liberally rubbed with oil, and—dressed in a cool swaying palm garment—he recites classical poetry set to music."

No wonder iron handlers have been regarded with tremendous ambivalence. The difficulty of getting close to them is due to the volatility of their material. Iron inspires awe and intense desire, but not intimacy. Even when Ogun becomes a finished piece, polished and oiled and articulate, he "recites" but doesn't exchange words. This is another reason women who come with these gods tend to leave. Passion draws them close to the fire. Oya carried the smith's tools in a calabash on her head accompanying Ogun to the forge, but then decides she wants his elegant, tricky and loquacious rival Shango instead. She steals away with him taking Ogun's divine tool, and runs through the forest with her new lover showering a trail of lethal sparks.

Training in standing close to the fire is essential to the arts of transformation—shamanic, alchemical, psychological or elemental. It is a well-published secret of the foundry arts, that "changes wrought by the fire are changes in substance." (Valery) Substantial change is a kind of torture. *Torture's* root is "twist" which is what the salamander, mascot of alchemists, does in the fire. Flame-twisted from red to green, the leaping creature signified the incorruptible essence of the flames. Your fiery salamander nature can not be harmed in the fire: "For it is he who overcomes the fire, and is himself not overcome by the fire, but rests in it as a friend, rejoicing in it." West African shaman-smiths called *nayamakala*—literally "life-force-handlers" led their sons to the fire in Camara Laye's experience described in *The African Child*. He explains the careful preparations his father made before taking him to face the terrors of the night fire. All the boys of a certain age are led—by constant fierce drumming, clashing gongs and fiery torches—into the forest farther than they've ever gone before. There, on the edge of the absolute unknown, they undergo the physical and mental torture of intense change in a short time, confronting masked fire-beasts who tell myths crammed with fact to inculcate manhood. The spirits then take the boys over the edge/ under Ogun's steel knife, sculpting them into men by circumcision. Like the ore-child in ancient metallurgical tradition the boy is violently extracted—taken away from the mother and the family—and thrown into a ferocious fire with charges of heat and blasts of fearsome inspiration that raise the psychic energy to the nth degree.

> brutal business
> making art
> flicking the wrist with precision

pouring hellfire back into the mouth of the mold. Like a father
with a sure hand
who claims
it's for your own good

It's an awesome transformation. A terrifying & ecstatic path to maturity.
The heat's on and turned so hot in the alchemical fantasy that the substance no longer recognizes itself, loses its internal structure and falls apart
chemically into other compounds. All that was solid gets destroyed in a
combustive flash that burns the gray-black boy to liquid gold, spurting
and then pouring out of the furnace in new and ungraspable brilliance.
Shadrach, Mischac, Abednego—and all the others—step miraculously
unharmed out of Pharaoh's fire.

When the moment comes for a particular piece to be poured, the artists
appear to stand alone. Their eyes follow the liquid fire and watch it slip
its dazzling silk into the cup of their mold. They know the hot metal's
required path intimately as if each dent and cleft and tunneled sprue vent
is contained in their own body. The final step of the transformation—
when the image is rendered whole and wholly new—is only complete
when the molten iron has traveled through every fraction of the internal
design. Some workers shout orders, insisting the iron progress in a certain
direction. Others urge on the pulsing course of lava silently. Like different
forms of prayer to the same deity. As each complex, hidden cavity is filled
and the welling gold backs up to broach the lip, the assembled crew shouts
in unison.

—"Do we have joy in this field?"

Yes! The iron pour resounds appropriately like a revival. It is a revival
of something ancient that is being reclaimed by these artists who feel

connected to the earth & air & fire & metal fundamental to the radical essence of casting iron art. Over our heads mostly bent to the smoky incubators that cradle the pieces, I see Ezra Pound's gospel unfurl against a cloudless sky. *Make it new.* What went in liquid and beautiful, beyond the boiling point in the imagination comes out solid, cool, harder than rock and ugly. Totally changed. Beauty kissed by the beast

WOMEN, FIRE AND IRON

University of Minnesota Foundry,
early 21ˢᵗ century, evening

Despite the brute strength required for handling the materials, the process of iron working is deeply feminine and is ruled by goddesses who dream in iron. Every night De-Meter, the Mother, giver of earth's gifts who was adept in the fire arts (but mistrusted by mortals), took the child Demophoön and placed him in the fire. Laying him in the hottest part of the fire "like a brand" she intends to forge him into something ageless the way a piece of wood is aged by fire into a torch. Or the way a piece of iron is made into immortal steel by heating it to constantly higher temperatures. The boy's name means "slayer of men" and he's a mirror image of another boy called "thrice plowed field" to whom the goddess teaches her arts of transformation (called The Mysteries) at the end of the story. Demeter deals with iron's duplicitous nature by showing how to change the sword into a plow. When this miracle was celebrated at the ancient Eleusinian Mystery rites outside of Athens in the year 480BC the signifying blast of fire scorched the sky for miles across the bay.

—You haven't lived unless you've seen the fire at night.

A woman in wild costume comes into the black yard. Her face is sculpted by fingers of light like the fire-swingers who danced on the sand in Puerto Escondido. They swayed in spirals of flame, holding ropes tied to buckets of fire flung in widening circles around their hips and high over their heads. Wrapped in a cobra print pareo, everything about her is smoke & fire, black & glinting. I've been to half a dozen pours now but this is the closest I've come to a nighttime pour. It's is a pyrotechnic celebration after a daytime foundry pour and reminds me of that first day in New Jersey where someone who loved the sparks of night fire told me the pour looked odd to her in daylight. Tonight there are fireworks and fire circles. Catapults, hoop dances and now this, a fire-swallower. She takes the flaming stick, tilts her head back like a maenad in trance, slowly inserts the flame into her throat, "swallows it" and draws the torch out again, on-fire. I'm as fascinated by her act as I am by her quick-change artistry. By day she'd been a foundry man like everyone else in jeans, t-shirt, chaps, apron and headgear. Now she's a goddess and wears the alluring, radiant persona of an extreme female fire-handler.

    one woman   only one   in dark eyes and visor
    looks on

    an artist
    she considers the advantage of cross-dressing

    as one way to get her tools back
    & closer to the operations

    acting the soror
    with its proximate thrill
    tricks her repeatedly into disguise

    now you see her
    now you see
    himself

    as the gods instruct

There are as many women starting out in iron now as there are men. What was once metaphor: woman as fire, iron mining as procreative, voluptuous furnaces fired by virile fire masters—has actualized on the foundry floor in transgressive splendor. Like a dream come true. What I mean is that the old gendered ways of imagining the process, its implements and materials, has become internalized common property in this new movement. A woman works with a vulcanic forearm to break up radiators for scrap while her iron-brother wears the helmet of Athena to dance in homage to the coal-pan. Mythic images always contain these crossover memories. To early metallurgists the work itself was conceived of as essentially sexual. Eighteenth century mining engineers (granted, Eliade is quoting the unique Novalis here) descended into the earth looking for ore, as if entering a mysterious womb, where "my beloved gladly comes to meet the works of my hand in the clefted dark." In the smithy the anvil was called the Bride..., which may be behind the phrase that survived into my childhood, "marriage is the forge upon which character is melded." No one talked openly in Protestant households about "glory holes" or the "sweet stream" of molten metal, but these current pour-phrases are all lingering images from an alchemist's vocabulary. In *Psychoanalysis of Fire*, Gaston Bachelard describes alchemy as a science engaged in by male bachelors, by men without women so that the process did not receive the influence of the feminine reverie directly, but rather indirectly in the projection of the *anima* (his female soul image) into the work. Consequently desire, especially unsatisfied desire, played a strong role in directing the transformative urge of the alchemist whose aim was to turn base common matter into something precious of his own. At the beginning of the Iron Age (on whose far edge we still teeter) the Greeks called iron *sideros*, meaning from a star, the same root as desire. The Sumerians called it *an bar*, skyfire, referring to the kind of heaven-sent iron that drops to earth in a meteoric flash. The Eskimo simply call it "Woman."

About ten years ago a group of women, local and international artists, used the university foundry to stage a pour for women, run by women. The irony of 'Fe' as the ferrous prefix for female was not lost on anyone that day when they gathered to handle hot metal together like a group of ecstatic Titanic midwives. Drummers sat on the edge of the foundry floor playing congas. Gigantic femme-fire puppets from the Heart of the Beast theatre hovered for the climax. Ceremonial artists constructed a vulvar furnace in the yard—to be lit and danced around in the dark. It's heart glowing red. The performative aspect of their work turned the entire pour into a conscious ritual that ended with the crowd, including men and children, following the looming Goddess in circles around the glowing furnace sculpture chanting "Everything she touches changes."

What kind of desire is it that fuels these gatherings? Earlier I suggested it was erotic. But it is spiritual too, this stirring of vital forces. Hexagram 49 in the I Ching describes the energy of the "Metallic Moment" led by the Queen Mother of the West. Her image stands for "skinning," as when the skin of gray sludge is removed from the top of the molten iron the instant before pouring. The glyph for skinning means *open above, radiant below* and is associated with the precise moment in the casting process when the gray layer comes off to reveal the transformed liquid metal. This is instant metamorphosis we are seeing—like the wildcat woman transformed by orange fire. Her moves are sinuous, unveiled, adhering to innate, repetitive form, calling us all to become her devotees. The I Ching says that the radiance of this fiery moment spreads outward in bright heat: "congregating people see and are aware."

Oracles have traditionally used a vocabulary of metal. In Greece the Sibyl sat on an iron tripod beneath the earth's surface uttering trance-words to her priests. Snaky tongues of smoke wafted her oracular words up from the cleft where she was stuck, mining for meaning. Once she gave the order that a certain stone of Pessinus in Phyrgia be transported across land to Rome. The stone was a celebrated meteorite hurled from the heavens (a *palladia*, as in Pallas whom we met before, Athena's playmate). Pallas also implies hurling and leaping girls / divine warrior maidens for whom thunderbolt tossing would be accomplished with the same ease as throwing iron spears. But this stone worthy of long-distance travel was said to be Cybele, a mother of the Dactyls and also the Phrygian Aphrodite. Aphrodite, the celebrity "wife" of Hephaistos, very likely started life on the planet as a sizzling hunk of fallen star.

How astonishing then, to see this woman tilting her head back to the night sky to receive a flaming ingot, God's rod that famously flamed in the desert. *When it's ripe and beyond bearing, Love goes to seed.* (-Creeley) Some desert peoples imagined the divine smith devising a fiery chain for the purpose of dropping an iron mallet to ground filled with seeds. When it smashes into earth's surface and settles underground, what's left of the iron mallet *cum* meteorite sits on a throne as if resting on the lap of Mother Earth where it generates visions. Iron seeds imagination.

At a cult site of Zeus Trophonius (called after a hero who was swallowed by the earth), those who came seeking visions were sent underground only after they had followed an elaborate preparatory ritual that rings true to iron's practical mythology. Seekers had to bathe in a cold stream (quenched) and take a (tempering) honey drink in preparation for the hardship they were about to endure. Pausanius described the ordeal of each initiate placed into the rock hole as if into a furnace. Once inside the hapless dark, a person spent three days in solitude barraged by reality altering images. In one instance an initiate saw floating islands in a nebulous firmament poked by two holes. Out of each cosmic hole vast rivers of fire poured onto the sea. Sometimes the moon slid over the surface of this sizzling chaos to snatch a drowning soul and lift it into her dim radiance, which meant that soul would get another chance on the dry land of life. Off to the side of the womb-like chamber where these visions occurred, a meteoric piece of swaddled iron rested on a throne.

Healing incubation required going into the foundry of earth's womb. Everyone at Trophonius had to go in feet first, reversing the birth process in order to be born again. You had to step intentionally into the heat. Initiatory demands—ritualized in stepping in and out of a circle of crimson flowers, or through a hoop of flame—ask you *to go through the hoops* of a necessary ordeal in order to alter the pattern of existence. It is very hard work, physically and psychologically excruciating. Endurance, Vigilance, and Steadyhand sit like sisters around the site of such sudden changes. The metal sculpture professor at the University foundry, who paced the perimeter of the women's iron pour, courts these sisters. He is eloquent in his insistence on the rules of casting procedure and regularly invokes the goddess Kanayago who stepped off a moon tree in southern Japan to deliver the treatise "A Secret Writing on Iron Mountain." Sometimes Kanayago is male, sometimes female. She wears rags and blackens her teeth. He travels with a dog who barks at him/her as s/he's descending to the moon tree from the back of a snowy heron. A foot gets caught, Kanayago falls and dies and sets up nightwatch by his/her own corpse. This watchful soul on top of a mountain of iron becomes the ancestor-god of all future metal workers. Her specialty is protecting from harm and increasing production.

—Every sense is immersed in utter focus. We're excited for everyone and totally reliant on each other.

The young woman talks about the paradox of iron's command: you are forced into extreme, isolating focus by virtue of the sheer difficulty of the work and yet there is an unspoken, complete reliance on your colleagues who provide collective support. They appear to be a rag-tag group.

46

Literally "rag", from *ragges*, a scrap rock, rough metalline stone resembling cast iron, and "tag", a shred of metal left on a casting that needs to be cleaned up. Yet, as in the case of Snow White's rough-and-tumble dwarfs, each iron worker stands in a particular idiosyncratic niche of the process that supports the working whole. Like separate fingers on one hand. Pot-bellied dwarfs surround her like Dactyls around Rhea suggesting that Snow White was once a goddess too. Long before Disney's white-washing she got split off from her witchy side the way our eye takes in the bright white face of the full moon never seeing its hidden side. In one variation of the story, Snow White only comes of age when she is able to condemn the dark Queen mother into the underworld, making her hop down the dungeon steps on a pair of hot iron shoes.

Cruel and unusual punishment, a constant in iron's realm, make sense in fairytales where the descent into the black void is indicative of a natural and therefore necessary event like the course of the moon across the night sky. It ends its journey by dancing downstairs into darkness. Only later, when the secret of transformation has been accomplished in the place designated *underworld*, does she dust herself off and show up again. Some of the women at the pour wear hard hats with day-glo double-axes sprayed on top. Moon insignia of the old goddess bless their heads with sharp ambivalence. Waxing (go ahead) and waning (watch out). Crescent signs point the way to the exhilarating furnace where, these women say, *we dare to use the body we've been raised to protect.*

FULL CIRCLE

University of Minnesota Foundry,
Johnson Atelier, New Jersey

Sitting in the sculptor's studio holding a slab of dense clay, I am left alone with a pile of tools and two double bladed axes that are bound to become part of a piece. I have carved a simple sand mold to pour a small plaque before, but this attempt to sculpt something that will be packed into a mold is different. Damp clay, smooth dry wood and cold acrid blade all seem on the far side of iron's heat. Oya's coolness next to Ogun's fire. Gradually my hands move with more sureness to make things happen along the shaft and around the blades of the ax. Wings emerge and a banded body and then a cluster of points like nail heads that I recognize when I see them two years later in a blacksmith's collection of Yoruban art. On a staff of Orisha Oko the neck of the stylized figure is fastened to the long body by a dense cluster of nails representing Oko's seed.

One of the love stories among the gods of iron tells about Athena's coming to the forge to request a new suit of armor from Hephaistos. He was attracted to her, wanted her on the spot and approached her impulsively for sex. She, with matched quickness, brushed him aside so that his arcing seed fell to earth. Into the underworld—where he can "make something of it." 'Making' is a many nuanced urge. Tension- producing, like the words fabricate, manufacture, construct, forge, cast. Words that shiver on the line between truth and fiction. You make it up, construct a story, forge a tool, forge a signature, and cast a thing in a certain light. This place, between art and reality, is precisely the home of Hephaistos. His other love, Aphrodite, the goddess of love herself, lived by the sweet wiles (*e.g.* deceitful stratagems, *synonym* artifice) of beauty. When Hephaistos successfully captured Beauty he was capable of the ultimate fabrication,—making *things come* to life. And

48

the other way also. When Beauty finds her way to the forge, she's able to turn her constant creative outpouring, her in-love-with-life overflow into something solid. Like the lovely star-maiden in Finnegans Wake who says "Wey, wey away, I'se so silly to be flowin' but no cannae stay," beauty's desire is to be stopped, and made graspable.

Products of the fire are modeled to be caressed. -VALERY

Magnetic attraction between Hephaistos and Aphrodite, between he-cast and she-molten, is like that between focus and dispersed flow. Opposed energies that strain to fly apart even as they are drawn to each other. The space between them is so charged that it needs to be ritually controlled—a job that belonged once to shamans & alchemists belongs now to artists who swear by the marriage of ecstasy and hard work. Ritual is related to routine as sacred is to mundane. A ritual is a formal procedure or ceremonial act that follows a customary order (you can count on it: rites, from *rit* as in arithmetic, are effective because they are imitations of the precise, orderly way things work). As in the knowledgeable Mande smith's *daliluw*—his stash of procedures for accomplishing things—you have to know origins to understand natural patterns. Elemental, developmental. Take the difficulty adolescents have in leaving home. Iron had such a hard time leaving the bosom of its mother, in the Finnish epic *Kalevala*, that it hid out for years:

> Iron lies sprawling in a fen, stretches out in watery places:
> it hid for one year, hid a second, forthwith hid a third, too,
> between two stumps, at the foot of three birches.
> But it did not escape by flight from the grim hands of fire
> ...
> Fire began to get bad, got quite horrible:
> it was just about to burn the wretch, miserable iron, its brother.

Ilmarinen the blacksmith was born at night with tiny tongs in his grip. The next day he made a smithy and on the third day he discovered bog iron in steely heel marks of a bear. One, two, one, two, three. Ritual certainty is cosmic arithmetic; first the flood, the fire next time. From iron's point of view the flood was of tri-color breast milk: the water of three virgins. Iron ore came from spurts of red milk. Steel from white. Bar iron from black that flooded the fen.

Proving his legacy by pulling off a one-man pour in the foundry yard, the white haired man wears his motto on his shirt: *Ferrum nostra non est ferrum vulgi.* "Our iron is not your common, everyday, iron." He and the other artists who tend furnaces of varying shapes and sizes consciously adhere to the alchemical dictum that insists on the mysterious nature of their activity. The fulcrum of their endeavor is planted deep in medieval metallurgical history where alchemy's liquid soul softened the hard mind of science. In fact it is almost eerie how much this pour scene resembles woodcuts in Georgius Agricola's *De Re Metallica* originally published in 1556. Hundreds of exquisite prints in that book show mine and metalworkers engaged in every aspect of their industry. Tools, furnaces, sheds, vessels, tanks, wheels, fumes, barrels—even lunchboxes and face kerchiefs—are richly drawn to reveal The *Development of Mining Methods, Metallurgical Processes, Geology, Mineralogy & Mining Law from the earliest times to the 16th Century.* Iron has an appropriately large presence in Agricola's tome. One of the woodcuts that reminds me of this long-awaited event happening in the Johnson Atelier foundry yard shows a man with his *arschleder* turned front, haired tied back, standing on a stack of slate to empty his wire charge basket into the top of the furnace. Chinoiserie clouds and tongues of dragon flame spew out the top. A monkish friend bends over the ore pile breaking it into smaller pieces with a sledgehammer. Two others stand at a table nearby taking a drink from a clay jar, talking with pleasure. It's a sunny day; the doors to the world outside are opened. The only difference between what I'm seeing in front of me and what's in the book is that all of the implements and structures in Agrico-la's exposition are labeled with block letters and helpfully identified below the frame: A) Furnace, B) Stairs, C) Ore, D) Charcoal.

'D' could also stand for demons. A man of science, Agricola did not want to linger long in their territory but he does point out that "demons are legion" and lists the ones who show up most frequently to plague pro-duction: mine-monks, shaft-spirits, trolls, gnomes, ghosts & dwarfs—es-pecially dwarfs. Even though they are short, they are part of iron's huge muscular imagination that has continued to plow through more recent centuries to the tune of John Henry the steel-driving man on one end of the scale and "hi-ho" the off-to-work-they-go dwarfs on the other. They all sing to establish the rhythm of driving work with a full range of sound from guttural throat thunder to the high-pitched kling of the extractor's hammer. Ironwork's demanding choreography, especially evident in this single-man operation where you get to watch one person doing each task in impossibly quick succession, keeps the muscled ones on their toes.

—*"Like his material, the mythical iron man was flexible and hard, pliable only when warmed. Otherwise strong-willed, driven, intractable & haunted. The beauty of the dance is that iron's devotee is moved by this ghost-river to follow careful rules & strict, repeatable, formal patterns of movement, always marked by precision in listening."*

Finally, I have found a voice in the theatre of iron. The Third Internation-al Conference of Cast Iron Artists has begun and I am giving the opening performance on mythologies of iron-handlers. Late arrivals wander in and out at the back of the huge tent. Hundreds of other artists lean in to listen. In a matter of minutes the organizers had built a unique platform to fit the intention of my talk that moves from prose's podium to a fire-lit stage for poetry. I like the anonymity of what I'm doing (I'm listed in the program as 'Nor Hill'). Functioning as mouthpiece for an iron god they know well.

—*"The beauty of this place, this particularly tribal iron-gathering, is in the deliberate reclamation of a foundry art that listens carefully to the voice of its material and to the voice of a culture nearing the end of an Iron Age. It seems no mistake that small-scale iron pours started popping up on the world screen at about the same time the tools of the Information Age began to infiltrate our lives for better or worse. According to the long view of the metallurgical historian, who can foresee the exhaustion of the world's fossil fuels, 'man's engineering uses of iron have probably peaked.' What he couldn't see is the movement of metal artists reclaiming iron's place, wresting it from the industrial forge, from large-scale to small, roots & all—returning it to a tribe that remembers its origins."*

In the penultimate paragraph there is a summary illustration of the iron-handler. Really it is mythology's portrait of Hephaistos colored by the dross of other, similar archetypal systems etched in heavy masculine hand. The nature of the audience required a standard, but to this group almost ludicrous (because accurate) disclaimer—that "any similarity to persons living or dead is purely coincidental."

—*"Iron-men are capable handlers, robust 'with sinewy hands and brawny arms like iron bands.' (-Longfellow) Persistent, hard-driving workers. In fact, Hephaistos is the only Olympian god who works! Workers are sweaty, muscle-bound, hunched, unheroic, abrasive, intense, crippled, bound-to-place, inventive, industrious, blackened, moody, ingenious craftsmen. Iron-handlers are capable of taking the heat, not talkative, slow to language, technical experts, practical and mystical, solitary. Engaging in no normal social intercourse, they can be found with other ironsmiths or in the company of their women who are literally helpmates or tool-carriers. Dark-eyed and heavy browed, angry at mother's rejection yet bound to her, obsessed with detail, in love with beauty, they are heterosexual but slightly inept. The iron-handler's loves conclude in disappointment, his art, never."*

As the giant mills close, the debris of a heavy-metal society mutates; steel plants are wired for rock band sound in northern England and the twenty six-furnace town of Falkirk changes foundries into offices in Scotland. Vast skeletal remains of brontosaurian blasters show sparks of life. In the Birmingham casting-shed turned art shelter, Ingot the Sloss Furnace foundry dog enjoys the company of artists-in-residence who use oil drums for mini-blast furnaces. In the Druisberg restoration project, ore-bunkers have been refit for rock-climbing and holding tanks for scuba divers. I imagine the proposed Smithsonian takeover of the collapsed Big Steel Lehigh River factory turning into a fantastic sound & light show. Flashing fire lights, crashing thunder and curtains of steam parting to pull us down in a molten swirl through a dark skulled ladle-pit into the pitch-black Earth Mother's lowest chakra. When your eyes adjust there are tiny gleams in the dark. Dwarfs rush along wielding picks that glint in her veins, gathering, channeling, stacking. Rolling along the glowing underground metallurgical river. They are all down there working: Dopey, the Dactyls, Orc, Diego Rivera, Athena, Vulcan, Hephaistos, John Henry, Ogun. Oya flirts dangerously with a sixteenth century chaplain of the mines while he preaches on properties of iron. Tolstoy's hunch-backed man on the iron rails eyes Anna Karenina. Walt Whitman swings a broadaxe. Gaugin remarks his preference for monsters of bolted iron at the World's Fair. David Smith's Terminal Iron Workers, the Rolling Stones, Nine Inch Nails, Spinal Tap, tap dancers, shamans, bards & bikers—they're all there. They would hand out 3D cobalt-tinted glasses and turn on a sound track of great bellows swelling music. The Anvil chorus. Hissing rings of operatic fire. Michael Mosi's flaming steel organ blasts sound into the cave. All in celebration of hands- on, hot and powerful art.

"Computer art ain't art if you ask me," the Newark taxi driver had said on the way to the conference. Is that why this small-scale Vulcanism is so arresting?

—*"We can't live without our fabricators, without the revolution from below that insists on handling the raw stuff of life, the vital force. 'True iron workers don't turn over the soil of cemeteries,' because they live on in what they pass on. Nayamakala, the ancestor says, a blessing on all that you blast and cast."*

—Hai!

Twenty some artists jam together in an exuberant closing circle after a daylong pour. Their rousing "Yes" is Japanese. The furnace design African. Their intention, alchemical: to find the extraordinary in the ordinary and force it out by raising the heat so high its waves make fall's tree gold swim. All iron has been poured, the air blast turned off and cupola bottom dropped to release a circular molten load of smoking debris onto the foundry yard. From the distance of outer space, slag remainder circles can be traced like running glyphs designating the spots where furnaces once stood. Sites of ecstatic transformation as completely "down to earth" as an orisha's dance circle etched in dirt.

There is bone deep encouragement in knowing that a natural material can withstand radical change in temperament, color, character, and form. The aging philosopher Bachelard said that images of iron gave him the "counsel of strength" to get up every day. He pinned three photographs of sculpture to the wall by his bed; "What a summons to morning vigor." Because of a secret aliveness contained in pieces supposedly *finished*, iron never dies. Rust is a sign of Ogun's ceaseless activity, even in death.

Iron always has another story up its sleeve.

ENDNOTES

"Works in the Invisible" in *One-Handed Basket Weaving*, Rumi's poems on the theme of work by Coleman Barks (Maypop 1991). Iron imagery runs through Rumi's poems. By "those generous ones" here, he is referring to the Prophets who ask "how long should we keep pounding this cold iron?" Cold iron is an unresponsive soul in need of a refining thrust into fire. He recommends handling by a great teacher like Abraham who wore fire for an anklet, Moses who spoke to the quenching waters, David who molded iron or Solomon who rode the wind:

> This one loves
> the ways that heated iron can be shaped
> with a hammer.
>> Each has been given
> a strong desire for certain work.

PRELUDE IN THE BOEOTIAN CAFE (PAGES 3–6)

Hesiod the possibly Homeric poet came from the Boeotian school of practical thinkers—not epic or romantic-minded, but down to earth and free of fancy. His coining of the Ages appears in "Works & Days" where he gives a practical warning to avoid obsessive stops at iron's door when there are things at home to be accomplished: "Pass by the smithy and its crowded lounge in winter time when the cold keeps men from field work,—for then an industrious man can greatly prosper his house..." Epigram X notes iron-smelting fires in the mountains. *Hesiod, The Homeric Hymns and Homerica*, trans. H. G. Evelyn-White, Harvard Loeb Classical Library no. 57.

FASTFORWARD (PAGES 7–10)

"The Third International Conference of Cast Iron Art," Mary Bates article in *Sculpture* magazine vol. 17, no. 8 (October 1998) describes the event that attracted more than five hundred sculptors from around the world. Held at the Johnson Atelier Technical Institute for Sculpture near Princeton, New Jersey 15-18 April 1998.

Mircea Eliade, *The Forge and the Crucible, The Origins and Structures of Alchemy* (Flammarion 1956). Source for mythologems. An exhaustive collection of relevant myths, rites and symbols that grace the liminal space between iron's practical workplace and its underworld of meaning.

Wayne E. Potratz, *Hot Metal, A Complete Guide to the Metalcasting of Sculpture.* (1992, Turtle Sign Company, 1104 15th Avenue S.E., Minnesota 55414). New edition forthcoming from Finney Co., Minneapolis, Spring 2017. A master teacher's philosophically grounded technical manual that covers metal theory and pour practice start to finish. University of Minnesota professor, sculptor and former art department director.

SERVICING THE FURNACE (PAGES 11–14)

Murray Stein's seminal article "Hephaistos: A Pattern of Introversion" notes that Hephaistos is the only Olympian God who works. Stein accounts for many Hephaistean habits originating in Greek myth, stories, epic poetry, language and includes an intriguing postscript on pathological and non-pathological elements of forging mythic connections to personal psychological material. *Facing the Gods*, James Hillman ed. (Spring Publications 1980).

Mr. Zipplers's furnace in *Casting Iron*, C. W. Ammen (Tab Books #1610, 1984). Chapter 4 describes the building of a cupola or domed blast furnace. The author approaches his topic like an animal tamer saying that "successful operation of any cupola requires not only a working knowledge of the beast, but a great visual, smell and hearing familiarity. You have to listen to it, look at it and into it, and smell it. It's no joke; this is all part of taming the cupola."

Life Force at the Anvil, The Blacksmith's Art from Africa. Tom Joyce exhibition catalog for The Artist-Blacksmith's Association of North America (ABANA) and the University of North Carolina at Asheville (1998). Ritual jewelry made for Dogon mother.

Pandora's story according to Hesiod, Theogony l. 567. See also John Layard's *Celtic Quest* second appendix on "Splitting Open the Head" (Spring 1975) Author discusses the intent of Hephaistos in Dactylic context, acting as midwife for Earth's birth.

Men tend a gynomorphic furnace mound with multiple vulvar openings in an ethnograph's photo illustrating "Origins of Technology" in a 1999 issue of *Scientific American*. Article by Francis Van Noten and Jan Raymaekers. The furnace was built in 1914 according to a design in use since the seventh century BC. It looks like the furnace meant by Eliade in chapter 5, "Rites and Mysteries of Metallurgy" where he quotes the Baila's song about finding the clitoris in the fanning of the flames. It sounds terrifying, but my guess is that the song is apotropaic, meaning that its intention is to turn away the desired thing that is feared: "Kongwe (clitoris) and Malaba the Black (*labiae feminae*) fill me with horror! I found Kongwe as I fanned the flames of the fire. .... Pass far from me, pass far, thou with whom we have repeated relations, pass from me!" Eliade notes traces of the comparison of fire and fusion with the sex act in songs, metallurgical taboos, and fire master's instructions.

Mining Lore, An Illustrated Composition and Documentary Compilation With Emphasis on the Spirit and History of Mining. Wolfgang Paul (Morris Printing Co. Portland, Oregon 1970). Facts of mining history related from inside one man's fraternity—of his own mind with the great iron struck minds of former times. Curious stories, hymns, and testimonies. His description of traditional leathern gear is like that worn by the gigantic sculptured Vulcan currently guarding the foundry museum in Birmingham, Alabama. Paul's text includes reverent biographies of scientists, kings, executives and priests whose life paths had ferrous significance.

Africa's Ogun, Old World and New, ed. Sandra T. Barnes (Indiana University Press 1997). Fifteen critical articles on the West African deity who manifests as iron in countless configurations. "Dancing for Ogun in Yorubaland and in Brazil," Margaret Thompson Drewal's piece on the power of utterance in spoken word and ritual dance, tells Ogun's hole in the ground story. Dancers express his self-destructive volatility in rapid cadence, ambivalent moves (thrust forward, leap back)—the gestures of war & danger. For the orisha of Ogun Cool and his pop-cult expression in the New World see Donald J. Cosentino, "Repossession: Ogun in Folklore and Literature" who covers the beat from Los Angeles to Brooklyn. Spectacular writing from inside urban hip apocrypha where iron's presence is coded in keys, chains, city fires, the road, force, palm wine, etc. Clearly visible sites of epiphany.

CHILD'S PLAY (PAGES 21–26)

The Gods of the Greeks, Carl Kerenyi (Thames and Hudson 1974). Childhood stories of Athena and Hephaistos. Primary myth reference.

Correspondence with Lyn Cowan, Jungian analyst, and teacher of alchemy who regards William Blake's payer, "May God us keep from single vision and Newton's sleep!" as a plea for avoiding fixation. In alchemy, iron was the most difficult element to deliteralize because Mercury (as in slippery, psychic Hermes) does not adhere to Mars (literal, fixed iron) except by artifice. Iron is by nature dogmatic and not reflective. What iron needs is the little red fox of Greek drama called the "iron" (sounds like eye-ron) as in "irony." Which is like telling a Cyclops he needs a sense of humor. In the language of the iron pour, *eye of god* refers, ironically, to the brilliant swirling center of molten iron in the full crucible. This is iron's least fixed moment, when the fluid gyre signifies an imminent reversal of state.

"In what furnace is thy brain?"   —BLAKE

See also Jerome Rothenberg and George Quasha, *America a Prophecy* (Vintage 1974). Blake's Orc in molten state breaks from his "mind-forg'd manacles" to rape the stony Virgin (body of America).

The Dream and the Underworld, James Hillman (Spring 1979).
Further notes on dogma. Reference in "Praxis" to the slowing down of Hephaistos whose bottom half is "in league with the underworld."

POTENT ARTICULATOR (PAGES 27–33)

Picasso and the Age of Iron, Guggenheim Museum catalog (1993) for exhibition curated by Carmen Gimenez. Anthology of Writings by the Artists at the back of the catalog features David Smith "Notes on My Work" excerpted from Arts 34, no. 5 February 1960. Tom Joyce (Catalog section "Forging Iron") tells an *eidetic* anecdote about the blacksmith whose teacher forged him a new hammer incorporating a small piece of his own, original hammer into it. And so on, each metal object containing memory of the past.

The Mande Blacksmiths Knowledge, Power, and Art in West Africa Patrick R. McNaughton (Indiana University Press 1993). Chapter 2 on the training of iron handlers includes breath-taking description of the arduous, musical—almost liturgical (in that the range of articulate rhythm can have collective, expressive function)—telos of apprenticeship. McNaughton's technical grasp and shaman/smith-like intricacy of perception are fuel for a poetics of iron. Text contains innumerable bits of illuminating information, like rods and cones in an 'eye of iron' proposed by Daniel Willis in *The Emerald City, Essays on the Architectural Imagination*, (Princeton Architectural Press 1999), "The Valor of Iron: An Introduction to the Material Imagination."

Joseph's story is told by W. Paul (*Mining Lore*) in a chapter of collected tales from pick-men in Germany. Illustrated spectral history of iron mines.

The Pirotechnia of Vannoccio Biringuccio, Classic Sixteenth-century Treatise on Metal and Metallurgy translated and edited by Smith & Gnudi (Dover 1990). Aptly titled classic treatise in language precise and palpable. The chapter on Ore is an Ode. Division titles like poetry: Assaying Auriferous Silver, Ways of Hanging Bells, Concerning the Small Arts of Casting, Melting with a Wind Furnace.

The Psychoanalysis of Fire, Gaston Bachelard (Quartet 1964). "Psychoanalysis and Prehistory: the Novalis Complex." A similar heat animates rock, a miner's heart and the poet's mind. With regard to the poet of the little blue flower, Bachelard says if you go deep enough into his dream of earth's womb "you will clearly see the truth: the little blue flower is red!"

"Wind & Sea, Fire & Night," Robert Duncan lecture in Buffalo, New York, November 1980. Published in *Opening the Dreamway*, ed. Robert J. Bertholf (Spring 59, A *Journal of Archetype and Culture*, 1996).

"The Dreadful God and the Divine King," John Pemberton III in *Africa's Ogun*. *Ijala* (poems of Ogun) and *oriki* (his praise names) printed in Yoruba and in English translation. See also Margaret Drewal on verbal performative dynamics in pronunciation patterns that contain/release Ogun.

SAVAGE & SOLITARY BEAST (PAGES 34–40)

"Saving American Steel," Doug Stewart for the *Smithsonian* magazine August 1997. Tells instructive grandmother story and revels in the beauty of the mills.

Story sources in Stith Thompson's *Motif-Index to Folk Literature*. Also M. Eliade. Interpretive depth psychologists Clarissa Pinkola-Estes, Marion Woodman, and Robert Bly work with the Baba Yaga's fire in various texts. Bly's *Iron John* is not really about iron, but the character does rise out of the swamp hole in rusty dreads like a clod of bog iron.

Sarepta oder, Bergpostill: sampt der Johimsstalishcen (Joachimstahl) (Nuremberg 1562). W. Paul mentions these sermons of Johannes Mathesius and translates the titles for them, hence my knowing about the Eighth Sermon which "concerns the kinds and properties of iron; where and how one digs iron-stone, smelts it and makes good out of it." Libraries hold copies of the original manuscript (University of Indiana) and xeroxed copies in old German script bound in Prague by the Narodni Technical Museum and Institute (University of Minnesota library). But no translations. I tried to find the Museum of Science and Industry folks in Portland, Oregon who backed W. Paul's iron project to see if his papers were collected anywhere. A past director and his secretary recalled the man, ("Has anyone told you he was eccentric?") but not much more. Actually, the ninety two year old Ines West was a sweet mine of information about iron in Oregon and suggested I search the State Department of Geology, to no avail. Mathesius is worth the effort—he who first said (in his sermons) "The apple does not fall far from the tree" and designed a fire engine to bring water up from the mines to the forge, in the 1560's.

Iron's lexicon: "Die Bergmannsprache in der Sarepta des Johann Mathesius," E. Gopfert, *Zetschrift fur Deutsche Wortforschung*, vol. 3 (1902)

The Tain translated by Thomas Kinsella from the Irish epic "Tain Do Cuailnge." (Oxford 1969) Tales of Cuchulain, hero and Hound of the Forge.

"Ogun, Builder of Lakumi's House," John Mason in *Africa's Ogun*. Real time documentation of Ogun in Cuba (1992) as reformed felon, rapist, addict: How to touch the white-hot rage/furnace burning in the gut in order to cauterize a grievous wound. With regard to Oya, Mason says "in her guise as tornado she blows houses apart for Ogun to rebuild. He can't stay away from strong women." (note 13.)

Alchemical Studies, "The Spirit Mercurius," (iii) Mercurius as Fire. Volume XIII, Collected Works of C .G. Jung, Bollingen edition (1967).

WOMEN, FIRE AND IRON (PAGES41–47)

Demeter's myth sung by Hesiod in the *Homeric Hymns*. The Eleusinian context described in my *The Moon and the Virgin, Images of the Archetypal Feminine*, "Mothers and Daughters" (Harper & Row 1980).

Women, Fire and Iron documentary short made in 1993 at the first women's pour. Lent by Wayne Potratz, University of Minnesota foundry reference collection.

Communication with Stephen Karcher, author of the new *I Ching, The Classic Chinese Oracle of Change*: the first complete translation with concordance, translated by Rudolf Ritsema and Karcher, (Element 1994).

Eliade tells the story of the Phrygian stone's oracular *translation* (i.e. how it was 'carried across'). Iron's divinatory function is widespread in cultures where paths of commerce and community intersect at the blacksmith's door. McNaughton among the Mande (chapter 3, on shaping civilized space) describes methods of divination: the diviners are the reason-seekers, ones-who-look, persons-who-know and they can speak the language of birds or snakes, throw cowry shells or stones. They draw word-images with a finger in fine sand on the floor of the forge and 'read' them for clients. Smiths make iron amulets, look into water basins for messages, fashion rubbing oracles. *Kilisi* secret speech is inscribed on a thin sheet of iron then washed off and swallowed or rubbed on the body.

Healing Dream and Ritual, Ancient Incubation and Modern Psychotherapy, C.A. Meier (Daimon Verlag 1989). Classical account, according to Pausanius, of incubation rituals at the cult site of Zeus Trophonius. The fact that iron appears as a bolt underground, probably a meteoric thunderbolt, is discussed in A. B. Cook's Zeus, vol. 1, I. 6. xxi. (Biblo & Tannen 1964). Cook's description aligns with David Smith's artistic certainty about iron's eidetic character. Attendants placed initiates in proximity to a draped rock altar or throne so that the chosen one got to sit on the divine lap (Mother's) and hold the power of the bolt (Father's) in hand. You would then get to be 'born where iron arises' which is another curious epithet for Zeus *Dolichenus*.

Of course the watchful presence of Endurance, Vigilance and Steadyhand does not always ensure success. When the fire master/mistress shouts, "don't dribble or overshoot" s/he's coaching the art of pouring iron.

Carefully aim the molten arc. Properly measure the angle of the pour. Too much too fast can cause dam bursts. Sudden trickles or floods of liquid metal gush out the sides of molds. Flames spurt from the top. (See Potratz' *Hot Metal Guide*, 1992) A few molds, like some initiates, are not fully prepared to handle the influx of metal and end up with a dangerous dispersal of uncontained material. It leaks out to puddle around them in insidious pools of orange fire. Shovels are instantly mobilized to rush loads of sand onto the spot. Occasionally the misshapen object resulting from a botched mold will be adopted as a piece of art and loved. More often it gets thrown back into the scrap pile where the iron grows cold and waits to be brought to life again, "deformed," as if it were the goddess Hera's rejected child.

Communication with Sanae Masuda. Kanayago appears in the *Secret Writing* (1784), a book on refining and metallurgical practices.

See also Lorena Babcock Moore, *The Ironwing Tarot* found after my initial writing of the book: www.mineralarts.com

FULL CIRCLE (PAGES 48–54)

Tom Joyce exhibition catalog. Figures 7, 7A & 7B, staff of Orisha Oko.

The Kalevala compiled by Elias Lonnrot in prose translation by Francis Peabody Magoun, Jr. (Harvard University Press 1963). "The Creation of Iron" (lines 29-104). Extraordinary picture conjuring: whortleberry boys, turnip headed warriors, iron fences wattled with reptiles, far-roving minds, cottage rows in Abodes of the Dead, squirrel coverlets, honey-toned horns, knives that gulp gore, tarry-prowed vessels, milk-rotten pines, sea bellows, flipping hammers. A preliterate stock of image morphemes.

Georgius Agricola, *De Re Metallica*, translated by Herbert and Lou Henry Hoover, (Dover 1950).

The Right to Dream, Gaston Bachelard (Dallas Institute 1989). See "The Cosmos of Iron." The pieces that inspired him were his friend Chillida's. There is no specific reference to the Dactyls, but according to Joanne Stroud's introduction other choices for titles were *To the Glory of the Hand* and *To Digital Destiny*.

END OF THE IRON AGE

(A POEM)

Iron, the best and the worst part of the apparatus of life.

—Pliny the elder

In view of the foreseeable exhaustion of the world's fossil fuels, man's engineering uses of iron have probably peaked. We cannot predict the eclipse of iron as man's premier metal, but we can predict the ultimate replacement of metals for some of the dominant uses today. We shall remain for some centuries in the Age of Iron, until the combustive use of fire itself is called into question by a future generation.

—Theodore Wertime

The smith usually works with several pieces at once to conserve time and fuel, and the alternating tasks of hammering and moving the pieces to and from the fire becomes very efficient as the smith finds the rhythm of the work and draws energy from it. This is an intense state of concentration that engages mind and body but frees the imagination.

—Lorena Babcock Moore

There comes a time when civilization has to be renewed by the discovery of new mysteries by the undemocratic but sovereign power of the imagination.

—Norman O. Brown

END OF THE IRON AGE

The poet thinks about male muses in her life. Beginning with Grandfather, the influential Protestant, who lived alongside William Carlos Williams and didn't know it. "Men still die miserably every day for lack of what is found there" as Williams said of poetry missing from newspapers. A black boy in New Jersey grows up to be a soldier in Viet Nam watching the divine hips of Oya dashing through the jungle. She runs with Shango when he seduces her away from the forge of Ogun—masterful god of iron. Following the trail of the god of iron constellates apocalyptic love dreams in girls who grow up in families that claim none of its men ever went to war. Realities about who goes to war, and why, come up on a trip to Lithuania.

I missed the chance to go to Baja with the North Beach poet who coined "spirit-meat" because I was afraid of being in a tent alone with two men in that desert appendix of the country. The other being an ethno-botanist from Tucson who came up with the idea. Life spirals clock-wise down the drain when watched closely. Of course it was sex I was afraid of not insects. Or, of not knowing what to say to the poet.

> living wild came easily on the edge of New York
> for a choir girl
> in bottle blonde hair
> black turtleneck & jeans

non-conformists
we all called ourselves
proud to think of marriage as a dying institution

the family contract was this
be busy
"count that day lost whose low descending sun
views from thy land no worthy action done"

next door to granddad's
the neighbor stood fake deer
a burro & two red-capped dwarfs on his lawn
declared tacky
& loved by children

our patriarch
the Reverend Dr. Posh
—Mr. Port Outbound Starboard Home—
wrote his books bundled on shipboard

plaid blanket, deck chair, bullion at ten
& one hundred letters a week

                                    March Eighth, 1964
Dear Eleanor,

Here are a few items which may be of interest to you.
   The one about the two versions of the film which was circu-
lated several years ago by the Unamerican Activities Committee
is very significant!

The longer article by a very good friend of mine is reveal-
ing and disturbing. It is the kind of thing President Truman
had in mind when he spoke of the Committee as he did: as itself Un-American. I shall be much interested someday to read
your report!

Lots of love,
Gramp!

postmarked Hackensack
several towns over from the place Williams died
after writing the long poem
that lies on its side like a woman

a park
in Paterson

lost on a corner in Paterson
my sister and I face a smoldering black boy palming a rock

he lowers his hand when we ask for help

(did Williams work nearby?)

riding bicycles the northern length of New Jersey
parched & frightened
my fingers grip black rubber too tight

Pater & sons

the boys will soon be dragged into another un-American war
reporting to the front
in the jungle where there is no front

so the war novel begins
with the young man driving
around &
around the lake
in summer

going in circles

preparing the first hoop of initiation

his heart heaves into emptiness

the doctrine of signatures says to read saplings
for a message
a rifle barrel rests its metal eye in the crotch of jungle tree
poking hard through tender foliage

Ayee ah!
Shango shakes palm fronds
making an air comb
whistle wind past Oya's hips

the iron god rages in the background
untempered
tearing after them through undergrowth
showering sparks

his eyes bulge
teeth grind
throat cords taut
hot & red, his rod
sizzles brown holes in the green

(all this visible through the soldier's gun sight)

Zsst! It sizzles and burns
blackened foliage behind him
zsst pssagh
monkey eyes dart
zsst
Ogun's poker glows orange-red to white hot.

> Senator Sir,
> We are concerned about the effects of
>   agent orange. Our boys are getting sick.

the protester's uncle heads north to the Catholic University
with one pompous hand still on his niece's breast and the other
            on the blackboard
                    he discusses Just Wars

Oya minds
her business

violent storms
seventeen kinds of wind
water currents
swaying
& balancing the cosmic smithy's

dark implements on her head
she dances away with her lover
wielding iron

her song goes according to the Latin night: first *concubia*
    time for embracing
followed by *nox intempesta,*   time of no action

morning is good
afternoon tempestuous
so she weaves it

Ogun darling
take your limp and shove
off

off our backs, like the bumper sticker after the war in Lithuania
translated by my jovial companion as "Russians keep your distance"
showing one stick figure mounting another from behind

first husband's first dream of first sex
he is rolling down hill
rifle bayonet sticking out everywhere
the round baker's wife opens a door & offers her rump

(my god you're only twelve!)

caught in his green brights & square-jawed grin
my belly squeezes shut
target
for his purring taunt—

It's just the butcher, the baker and the candlestick maker
hey baby, don't you like it like this?

as I was saying Ogun
you are my next of kin, my nightmare
too close for comfort
too distant to get a new name

thinking about you others occlude you
you with bulging muscle
trying tenderness
steeped in blood
you are the white-hot pillar of love
plunged into woman waters

to name a place steeped in legend is tempting
or to say its people   Dogon   Ashanti
                    Balkan   Tibarene
geography rearranges itself along this fault line

you raise your sword
you are the enemy
you will slay the enemy
wind roars
lightning cracks

when you spew your gasoline
rage hacks ancient trees into charred coal

jealousy flares
birds fly straight up

squawking outrage to ozone
as I say this to you from the other side of the fire
    bellows-mate
            ground-thunderer

the town disappears into darkness
its lights beneath us, stars

a dream

Incredible star showers. We stand by the guardrail. Leaning into the warm
belly of the poet I point out the orange sparks proliferating too fast, too many.
Suddenly the Cosmic Explosion! All goes black. We can run directly across
to my brownstone but instantly it's darker than ever before on earth and cold
cold cold

the poet was CoalMan sharing the body of a man called Star

a fragment of Ogun's wild hammering imagination, I am
watching sparks fly from the anvil of night

this is the End of the Iron Age
the world as we've known it skids to a stop

    wherever "suddenly" appears you know a loosened god
    like Mars or Dionysos or some comparable
    non-Euro riproarer has entered the room

watch out for shamans in drag
who will scoop out your insides

muttering *kilisi* words
& gesturing
open wide!

it hurts when a god enters

swollen too big
too many words inscribed on the rim of the bowl
washed with rainwater
& poured back into mouth

amulet preparation for the deranged

O prophet
take it back
lie down and take
this cruel history lesson
in god-snarl
back

how he has his own one hand on dancing balls
and with another taps his chest
testifying to eternity
victory gone berserk

Ogun strikes
Ogun shatters
Ogun scrapes

in his grass skirt
in his skirt of palm
in his palm
palm nuts rattle

wood in hand
iron in hand

he pulses & expands
three times his hot size

his tool is sharp
ai-ya!

no other god can approach him in the bush

Ogun cleared the way
    16 paths
    for 16 sons

at the beginning of time
my first love-path led to a priest
then a poet
then the shamans
no soldiers anywhere in the picture
not a warrior among them
cross my heart

only bards as ancient umpires
stomping feet on holy ground
divine warriors in a dionysian camp

fought wars with wine
and won

but look who tears across the bog
Cuchulain in a warp-spasm
arrows of fire bursting from his head

women and children take cover in politeness
excuse me! excuse us! coming through!
when really
they are desperate to get out

men cower
Cuchulain sputters and terrifies
his rage one hundred bladed
shining blind
smoking black
flack
 ash
 cinder
shelled
he explodes into every cell
of her I-swear-I-didn't-choose-him body

lying to one side on her pyre
the mother smolders

her belly a crater
gaping fist hole
purple as far back as he reached
to empty her of child

boy
oh boy
man oh man
Jeez
Jesus H. Christ
God!
see? every one male
shit?
well
you don't hear girl oh girl
or
woman
its always "man" this "man" that
our daily ejaculations
yeah

It's too cold to go down into the basement for proof that I lied about never choosing the warrior. I know there's a letter still: Erik Scott APO somewhere near the Great Lakes. A fierce English teacher warned me, never change him, "he's the only Huck Finn I know."

as soon as he signed up for the service
I shipped out
despite the ache
in my belly

who do you want Oya?

is it Shango in elegant shade,
or iron-limbed Ogun oiled and flickering
in intense heat
THIS IS NOT MY WAR

Dear Nor

Iron is for me an emblem of stubborn strength, grit, at
times, grim determination which can be used in the service of war or healing. When I was courting, I dreamed of
honey oozing through a red iron door.

Mr.mythos@X.net

Sweet seep—
a security leak
when her sluice is locked against love
by iron will

not serving war
or healing
but in service to a marriage ruled by Mars

the battle of love-mad bees
swarms to her grate
fills the Carmelite opening
with crazed words
iridescent wings

black & gold warriors
swoop to elude death by taking aim

furious at being held back from the source
the honey makers surge in sickening
thigh high waves
oozing toward the sting

In Nam, man, they had gook bees the size of dogs.
You wouldn't catch me bloodying my spear on one of those bitches.

MY BROTHER'S KEEPER?

Dying before he turned fifty, the poet's Hephaistean brother David comes back to help her work on the problem of artistry and craft. She accepts an invitation from a sculptor in New Jersey to think about iron in order to eulogize David. The Dactyls come to life. Ogun rears his head. Every time she tries to get to the subject of the use of iron in art, the material insists on veering off toward war. Loveliness incarnate rises from the sea and wants the very man who repulses her. Aphrodite's desire is to make love to war, but it's Hephaistos she marries. He can fight if he wants to, with blasts of fiery wind like a hot typhoon, but he's more interested in Beauty. She is appalled by his ugliness. But the greasy, bearded, limping muscle man hunched over the forge draws her like the other end of the magnet. Apparently it's the gods decree that enemies attract. The poet benefits from the instruction of Sakhan shamans and the elder poets, roof-weaver and beach-walker.

Brother of wet dreams
& unclaimed children

I see you at the heart of the kiva
standing with arms around your wife
making sounds together
visible puffs
rising toward God

you followed
soon after
through a hole in the top of your skull
crushed in the truck slam
     no helmet
your dual-cylinder cycle sideways on the road

David

she said you'd awakened with stars in your eyes
that very morning

quiet strongman
your hands speak
make rings
caress ivory
cast bronze

iron-hammerer
gripper of tools
you rose from the work bench
to follow young women's hips
passing at eye level
all that sweet coming & going
gone

How did you escape the war? Brothers, father, grandfather, uncles, one hus-band—how is it that the chinks of no-battles fell so precisely to accommodate the men in this family? One boy only crossed enemy lines on a horse once to alert Camp Washington that men in red coats were coming long ago.

now amorphous wars with no borders
slither into our guts
sucking cousin-blood in Cambodia
& strewing skulls
on holy stone

piles of empty bone
mock the master of inquiry in renaissance tallow light
staring at a single skull. Whose?

damn my ignorance

I miss the centaur I once married
hirsute answer-man

ex-marine, (another warrior)
handed a government check for books
his library grew
& grew with the weight of Gutenberg's progeny
philosophers classicists mystics madmen

our fingers tapped in unison
on the spines of those books
companions
in our solitude

his memory was photographic for text
zero for context
ask anything:

who held the skull at arms length?
what was Creeley looking at?
where did A.B. Cook quote the temple sweeper?
what is the Latin root of desire?
is Inanna at the 6th or 7th Gate right now?

constant crisis fueled
the imagination

Sunday   descent
  Monday   descent
    Tuesday   descent
      Wednesday wandering-as-if-dead
        Thursday   eat dust
          Friday   dry sex
            Saturday   dream ("The Lord of the Underworld
Also Has You")

  underwater   clear down
  but not too far down for my eyes to grasp
    a pencil "Ceres no. 2"
  rests on a massive stone lintel

writing will be my ticket
to the bottom

know what I'll give you when you get dead?
what?

my daughter holds
lamb's wool
& a gray stone taped together

the nest

you get the nest
Dad gets the stone

hard & soft
held together in a child's mind
as by the hand of an artist
who carved Voluptas
to fondle
& placed her next to a meteoric stone
everyone knew
was Eros
descended abruptly
in the climax of night sky

I loved my brothers

long before one got dead
I took them lemonade in the backyard

even when I swung from the rungs of the jungle gym
landing squarely in their sand kingdom
a gigantic Athena
burying plastic soldiers
battle lines demolished

even in the face of their fury

At least one theory of angels
says the dead
appear as shooting stars—

this is how it happens

   a god betrayed by a mortal lover

        (loving god is a death wish
        sweet longing to be thus sparked
        come o come
        with your raging bull's foot,   Come

        charging down this furrow

        a sacred act he says
        & she goes along with

        until he sees she has a husband
            or child to attend, so

     arranges her dead
     he throws her towards her hook in the sky
        where caught & splayed & studded
     a wary constellation
     still shines

I have been unfaithful to my teachers

careening from field to field
trying to locate stepping stones
intentionally placed
beneath placid waters

I have been unfaithful to followers
I did not like

moving
gingerly toward Trakai
        red-roofed castle in the moat of a gray lake
her trees trimmed to hard ground
in order to observe foolish enemies testing
the Baltic mirror

I found the steps myself
and did not turn to tell

here and here

I have been unfaithful to Classics the Ruler
I confess I claimed insight
by means of imaginal etymology

Father once tried to follow my derivation
from demure to demur
& declared it erroneous

your fault! I was inclined to say,
you sat with my brothers at table
declining Latin verbs
when I was underage & awed

the rigid patterns rang in my ears
shaping a girl's refusal to ever learn that way

instead of walking the line
dance around it
the good Swiss doctor said

& led me along the spiral path
showed me hidden storerooms in Pompeii
held a mirror to the dark of the moon
breathed with me through labor

when I'd already left him for another lover!

to thine own*selves* be true
the other one said

coming out of the clearing

when I turn to look back
he is on top of the house
weaving a roof of forget-me-nots

nor will he be
ever
forgotten

on the long road
shedding jewelry
the crown
the aegis
the breastplate
the girdle

down to this remnant

mid-stream
I stood on my own
   & fell
hitting a rock in shallow water
bone clang like iron
struck
head to anvil
sight-blacked
dead?
no
but pierced

a third eye
rock-struck & red

on the gurney in scrutinous light
the doctor's gaze strips me
essential. Why now
this violent recall to Blake's warning

"beware single vision and Newton's sleep"

   drifting

        Eleanor & so-and-so
        kissing by the gate
        love is blind
        but the neighbor's ain't

        A - B - C - D - E - F   Frank!
        "un uh
        Ford
        last names count,
        it's Billy Ford"

   jump-roping my way
   toward the nine year old
   fireboy around the corner

Love is supposed to be blind
seeing not with the eyes but with the mind
veiled
until a shade on the inner eye snaps up

Honk if you believe

& step into an indigo night
when only wolves could see

a heavy figure slips along the stream
a-welter side to side
whoosh
she feels her waters gush
warm on to her thighs

on her knees
with no care for rain or wind
straining the body's full length
—dangerous exertion behind the eyes—
she pants to push her insides out
in a screaming velvet crown

where her fingers clutch the earth
the mountain brought forth
as many spirits as the Mother of Gods had fingers
ten Dactyls

iron-fingered blood-brothers
sorcerers on one hand
smiths on the other

ten magical artisans
clustered at her side

ancient mountain diggers
wide-girthed earth's own muscle men
pick & chant

chant & sing a sound
that bounces along highland ridge
rides the wind spire down to town
to lodge in the chest of a boy
learning to work
the bellows

Dear Evan,
c/o Minneapolis Institute of Arts

In further pursuit of my thoughts about iron, I am digging
around in the archetypal territory of Hephaistos/Ogun and
note that in those early systems there was no distinction
between mental & manual labor i.e. the craftsmen were
called "pre-eminently intelligent" in the same breath as
the high gods. What I need now is to know more about the
history of the split between artist and craftsman.

Looking up
I see
trees
turned to wrought iron

filigreed branches
pressed flat
against sky

it's a balmy winter day
snowdunes like frozen cream
up to my breastbone

strips of flamingo and turquoise
tear across the sky

a lone crow

I have seen it

etched in leather on the back of the Sakhan shamaness
who turned slowly
arms outstretched
performing endless rotation

    riding the coldest current
           she cawed

chills long as her braids
run down our backs

comrade shamans make the ground erupt
in whistle and click of tundra
real enough
to hush a crying child

conjuring crickets & elk & the moon rising sound

down from Yakutsk
the shamans come
bringing their nine sounds made in nine parts of the back
passed on through nine generations

wandering
in the hot scented night the youngest male
drunk & bellowing
pounds on women's doors

She-who-sings-in-her-sleep startles awake

drawn by her sounds
he is lost
stunned by the Provencal fortress
standing seven hundred years strong
when his people live in houses
of moss
& wood
rebuilt every twenty

drunk on fire-water, he burns
his thread to home
the elder warned: no alcohol

but the boy bangs his bottle
against the one familiar face he finds
plank door, rough wood, iron latch

crying
to escape
the iron-beaked Mother
Bird of Prey
in Yakut proverb
"smith and shaman come from the same nest"

even her feathers are iron
and black black her heart
that tears these boys apart

no chance operations
she proceeds in order:
scrape flesh
cleanse bones
reassemble body
fasten with iron

a magical power boy
rocked back to life
in a heavy metal cradle

it's all in the rhythm

... news to me
to be gripped by images
so alien

the beloved professor once
socked me father like
saying, *you don't read
the paper*

now I read
front page news from the Iron Range

Thursday   January 16, 1997

Two Survivors of Runaway Train Amazed They Cheated Death

carrying a load of iron ore
ninety three cars headed for a steep bluff
down a seven mile grade to Lake Superior when the brakes failed
clouds of snow slamming metal flying four inches above the track
purple pellet dust exploding

O god of train wrecks
alert at the switch

set apart by physical defect & oddities of accident
the mythical metal worker lurches from burning cave
coming down from the hills

   his breath is fire
   his glance a blaze
   condensed
   not luminous
   or heavenly

   looking at him
   I stare into a furnace

dynasties change

Once-was-a-god slips
into the role of overseer
patron of new work
        knife-grinders
        cab drivers
        steel workers
        mechanics
        railway men
        night watchmen

praying together for protection from accidents

yea
who shall protect thee from accident of birth?

sometimes Snow White chooses
the dwarfs over the Prince

   really mom! it does happen!
   poop was white in the olden days!
   (I say nothing)

odd men in a hurry
pant & puff
pupphusa-h (Sanskrit)
phnut-phunt (mid high German)
poipnuo poipnuo (Greek)
bustle-breathed scuttling crab-men
whistle while they work

Hephaistos is the only god who works

mother said she would only marry a man
with savings in the bank
Homer worked
had the savings
and the opera tickets
to make it a go

they didn't know about the
unlived queen, how Hera-in-her would

    step aside   (she smote the earth with two hands)

    and create on her own   (she felt Gaia quiver)

    a son

foundry foundling
fell
for the length of a day
to crash
lungs smashed
on the isle of Lemnos
barely a breath in the bellows

Ogun wants in here
   he thinks any mention of hard
   breathing belongs to him
   iron-lunged fire master

after all he hears the sea nymph calling
oh Blastbreather
how should he know she means
Hephaistos
that other forge lord

god of hard hats
construction zone artist

you know beauty when you see it

rosa ragusa lines the beach
pink-pistils quivering

loops of seaweed
undulate in shallows

then (the scene required it)
a woman rose
from the metallic sea
nipples hard & dripping foam

Botticelli!
the rhapsodist interrupted himself in mid-sentence
to notice her

we all noticed her
in the flash of setting sun that cuts across a beach
belonging to nudes
north of Santa Cruz

perhaps the difference between a mortal beauty and a goddess is that the god-
dess doesn't feel her beauty a burden

the scribe takes notes
in the act of noticing her beauty I side with the onlooker
what if I were pen & stylus twins on either side of Sumer's queen
when she rose up
from hell not ocean
but still
beauty
so awesome
it silences

silent in his own way
my brother's voice sank
soft and low as moss

the Protestant side of the family couldn't make an opening
for him to tell us about love
so he brought our attention to his sculpture

articulate dancer
long-limbed loose-haired
gracefully seated in lotus posture
for eternity

after her crowning at the art fair
I drove your Pandora home
along route 17
from Chautauqua to New York

my Ford wagon blessed

reaching a tangle of garlanded cars
heading for Woodstock
she received wild acclaim

"O perfect artifice..."
pelted with food & flowers
your first love smiled at drunken offers
to come along

we inched toward the intersection of an age
hidden in that hot summer jangle
an impossible knot of roads at crossed purposes

do I deliver my brother's art
or dare the detour
into my own?

the Virgin beside me proved a tricky burden
Fate placed with forethought
& her typical flair

III
ZILLAH'S LAMENT

At a certain age all children are prophetic. It's difficult to understand why the teachers tell the second graders complex stories about Good and Evil but then take all the black crayons out of their boxes. Cain is a black mark. Iron is black. A blacksmith wanders into the poem from the African desert. One of the brothers. A shaman-smith who could handle the dangerous nature of the material. On the one hand a friend of mankind, his is the stuff of ritual art, agriculture and adornment. On the other, killing. The only woman who could ever find her way close to his furnace is a woman disguised as a man. Metallurgy claims an essentialist's reason for this: that the ore and the furnace are female. A forgemaster's feed-the-fire energy would be distracted by the presence of a woman. Hence tom-boys. Strange but predictable outcome of the desire to see for yourself. All the lights in Seattle go out when Richard Serra forges Snake Eyes and Box Cars. The sun of the last sentence goes down on the poet's marriage to a teenaged warlord.

My child hums and paints
standing at a kitchen easel
in the morning light

eyes intense
hand steady
her hum broadens into words
that curse the canvas

"Whirl of wind
with fire of grief
When the bomb comes through the world
it will look like this!

Hum of Heaven
Gates of Iron

THE END!"

echo of Job
flung by terror through the nightwind whirl

the same hissing God
stood the first couple up
in a waist-high garden

in a land of milk & honey
they wobbled on iron stones

ground litter
ultimate treasure
dropped
to earth

God's gift of skyfire
meteoric iron *an bar*
      called Woman by some
           or desire burst *sideros* from a star
               slammed to the ground in a flaming
hole

dark & rich & malleable

brothers fought over her
raised their hands against each other
hard enough to kill

one brother dead & the other
banished

centuries later
desert people still ask
how Cain made his way

full of rage

    he walked away from a star

        so heavily

           his heart hardened

at every step his darkening fantasy
considered ways to use her

trembling from the bottom of his spine
hip-shook & hauling his bucket of pelvic fire
he pictured hammering
heard own throat-thunder

obsessed
with what he could make her do

when he reached the Land of Nod
half-dead & deafened by roaring skull

he stopped

dregs of a wanderer's desire filtered
through generations of settled sons
son to son & so on
until three decisive vessels were uncorked & poured

Jabal   Jubal   & Tubal

shepherd, bard, and ironsmith

and Woman?

at long last she was known
by Tubal-Cain the strong man
who wrapped one arm around a lamb
and with the other strummed her lyre

Interlude
Cast, Beloved (David)
    Rich-in-Sorrow (Deirdre)
        Messenger-of-Light (Eleanor)

*Once upon a time on the pilgrimage road to Chimayo north of Santa Fe
with Beloved and little Rich-in-Sorrow, Rich-in-Sorrow picked up a large black
rock outside the sanctuario. She held it in her two hands as long as she could,
knowing that this was holy ground and the rock must be special. Beloved,
Messenger-of-Light, and others take turns carrying it when she grows tired.
They grow tired and leave the rock by the road until the trip back from lunch.
Tears of protest. Followed by assurances. Beloved : " It is a magic rock and
nothing will happen to it." Rich-in Sorrow reluctantly agrees. When they return, the safe place had gone haywire. Messenger-of-Light cries out: "Medu-
sa!" The black rock so carefully placed under dry grasses against a utility box
was covered with an explosion of untouchable wires, a nest of neon vipers.*

Ordinary objects from the house of childhood endowed with *an bar*

    rocks

          knives

        axes

  hoe

    nails

          hinges

  andirons

            waffle iron

    boot scrape

              furnace door

      cast iron skillet

each with their own story
like the iron stove who saved a troubled boy
by listening

(iron takes impressions)

    he tells the stove
    his secret
    slipping it into the scene securely cast on her iron breast
        a hand's-width cottage, lamps aglow

    in the story's end
    truth prevails

    but we (listeners
    inside the fire) know
    in truth
    imagination prevails

Sons of the sons of Zillah and Cain I overhear news of you at my husband's company party. How a brother signed up for war but went to the foundry instead in the footsteps of his father, to be useful, to make money, to be a man and how it happened that he was crushed in that place, that became a hell place, by an elevator. The day before reporting for active duty.

    Woe unto the youngest metal
    Iron ruled by Hades

tacking down Rigg Street on a drunken night
another ghost of Cain returns

I prepared a room the way mothers say

a fresh bed

&

even if it's on the floor

a reading lamp

a single flower

which bothered the other women

who wanted to know
(all things being communal)

would you make it
tidy & welcoming like this
for a woman?

Yes

       young man of Samothrace
     ringlets waxed short
        your skin olive taut
   shines through the grease

black oil   biker grime   a bull-dancer
or   at least   a maker of bronze
jewelry for bull-dancers

with a name like Toad
and a dog called Puck

he bellowed his way home at 2 a.m.
kicking a skillet before him

the morning part is not clear
except for an angry house
and a gray body-print
on yellow sheets

I disguised myself to go along with men

using names that pass
    for tom-boys in the '50s

Robert
Jack

had I known
I would have been Zath-Sparam
            Vulcan   Numuw

brothers climbed into the furnace to scrape out ashes
built ecstatic fires to melt coins

dug into earth to leave time-capsules
construct a club house
& christen it the SLY FIVE

a sister could only wear the scout uniform

now I wear the bohemian artist's outfit
try the welder's gown
learn to drive the bus
    double-clutching over mountains
but the fact remains
    boys can piss out the door of a moving bus
    and I can't

cunning makes me an apprentice in this desert
where brothers talk in trade secrets

their coded calls
pierce still air
circle the earthen furnace
& penetrate the inner ear. Words
magnetized by affinity
clamp on their night mail
to rush the primed dark

one man
fresh from the mine
walks
bent low
nuggets of sound
caught in his beard

the frightened apprentice I hide myself in
stands close to the callused hand

a black hand with missing finger
that reached for ore
according to no map but stars
that led through the mountain cleft
down a marked hole

no wonder people think you are part god

no recesses are secret

....even in the bowels of the earth

your name is shit-man, trash-collector
bloated, crawling-in-it-one
fetish-concealer
hiding beneath filth

nayamakala

treasure in the fetid ruin
ripped out

loaded onto lithic shoulder

borne through wilderness
through power places
where night demons are flattened in the wake of his push
towards fire

a brother (as Jabal is to Tubal)
collects the nuggets from around your mouth
he, bard, is your word-smith
and you, his ore-man & necessary smelter

What are you going to be when you grow up my professor wants to know, of-
fering me a hand as I step from the dissertation fires. It seems clear, had I been
born in the 19th century: a missionary adventurous & kind & living in exotic
places. OK, saved from that fate by time, now what?

a scribe

I act the scribe
whereas I want to be
but would never say it

a bard

finding words
scattered on the ground
bringing pellets of pyrite to the flame

prima materia words
        like   persuasion
           pharmacopeia
               purpose
            planetary
                  pulse

whispered over charcoal
in the dark of a particular moon

the firemaster
cuts the slag hole
stacks wood
draws the bellows line
stretches goat skin
sonorous

tamps the ground
carefully
as if preparing for birth
the implements are laid out
openings checked

the apprentice sets the rhythm of the bellows

foo oo ah foo oo ah foo oo ah foo ah foo ah foo

a ritual blast
blessing before
cursing behind
it's time to charge

5 hours
10

foo ah foo foo   foo ah foo ah foo   foo ah foo ah foo ah foo

40 hours
72   until the red clay episiotomy
tapped by the tender
enlarges her hole
to match the silver slit of new moon

appearing wider ever wider
she eases out
a shimmering mass

*In a far western region of Mali iron was still being smelted in the 1970s.
A Peace corps volunteer reported that at the end of the procedure a 200lb
piece was dragged steaming from the furnace. Blacksmiths poured water over
it to cool it down and townswomen came forward to lift their skirts and absorb
the vapors. Others collected the liquid after it had cascaded over the iron and
drank it*

aroused by metal
& warmed by spirits swirling in crystal
women
half-way around the world
tap a rhythm across hardwood floors
to praise the artist's performance with gallery words
    bold!   architectural!   original!

    Splash Piece: Gutter Cast Nightshift (1969)

making waves of molten metal
the Night-Caster flung it from a bubbling cauldron
bands of bent material scalding and cooled
pulled away from the all night wall in leaden waves
wave after wave

brutal business
making art
flicking the wrist with precision
pouring hellfire back into the mouth of the mold. Like a father

with a sure hand
who claims
it's for your own good

once the entire city of Seattle groped its way through a blackout
in capitulation to art's desire

all energy doomed to the suck of Jorgenson's forge
demanding every kilowatt
slurped into its maw
higher & higher
to the thousandth degree
heating toward the penultimate blast
the sun turned red
& the moon turned black
when the hammer smashed
his block of fire. The artist roared his orders
along a crimson edge
hotter & harder to slam the molten pillar square

steel more dense than any made by man

24 tons each on the back of Ogun again:
massive shiny chromed flat-bed haulers
the largest blunt-cabbed monsters of efficiency west of the
Mississippi
groan under the weight of their single stone, a procession
to take the sculpture home

it is a man's world
in the company of Jack-the- forgemaster,
artist, truck drivers & construction workers

one woman   only one   in dark eyes and visor looks on

an artist

she considers the advantage of cross-dressing

as one way to get her tools back
& closer to the operations

acting the *soror*
with its proximate thrill
tricks her repeatedly into disguise

now you see her
now you see
himself

as the gods instruct

old bristle-beard Thor
got his tool back
by draping Freya's veil
over his hot head

a milk & salmon fed oxen-sized bride
he was bustled into the throne room

glaring through lace at the idiot traitor
who dared woo him
as a her

he hid his iron gloves in the bulging lap of the bridal costume
and held them still with the clench of his will
until bedtime
when the dim-witted Thrym
ordered the god's hammer
(Thor's stolen bonk & banger)
brought in to bless their bower

instantly the tool recognized its master and the scene
unveiled its fury
cracked skulls rolled above
& thunder storms below

in the thrash of wedded foes
Freya's borrowed veil floated
across the sun

& people walking in the glow of the Bronze Age
found themselves cast in a grim swath of gray

eerie ire
in dark of night
no show, no gold
fini

Nor & Thor went out to watch the sun rise
one honeymoon dawn
over a pinkened lake

any minute now
a hot gash on the horizon
but
then
the sun slipped under an anvil cloud
& was

gone

IV

QUEEN OF COOL AT THE
GATE OF DAWN

Attending to her own dreams in a long weekend with a Mayan shaman who prescribes traditional dances from Guatemala, the poet meets her match. Thrown into the ice age of her ancestry she reconsiders the nature of grief and maturity. Things get quite cold. World sisters come to her aid. In Lithuania she is taken to the pilgrimage site of Our Lady at the Dawn Gate in the city of Vilnius. A fire lit by the shaman flares up in a dream defense of Agla the mail-lady who is running for parliament. Inquiries are made into the role of iron in Baltic mythology. Unprecedented tears pour into the subterranean realm of the dwarfs who carry war stories to the grave.

Cruising above our heads
the eye of jaguar shaman
searches the crowd

his gaze hovers & catches
gathers immense power to itself
& dives
straight into mine

chosen
to do my dreaming out loud

as he listens
I begin to hear
ice in a frozen harbor
cracking up

jagged slivers of violet light
cut through
the solar plexus
polar cold
where heat's intended

    RX: a bundle dance

ice woman
meet man-on-fire
the jaguar says
you two need each other

he binds us with drumbeat & prayer
sends us dancing in a slow circle

side by side
we shuffle and bend
awkward
until the melting starts

his is the too-hot of the great Grandfather's chair
going up in roaring flames

wild lion fire licks out of a dark alley
& roars down the street encased in steel
rage music bursts his lungs
fighting fire with fire & screeching sulfur
his fuse is short

lightning-rider
crouched
by the treacherous campfire
in a fairy tale forest
no longer safe for children

he has a fist of fire
a tongue that terrifies
iron-jawed man
carbon forged by constant
thrust
into burnt coal
thrust & hammered thin

steeled for conflict

his own fear turned fury
to this deadly edge

when the furnace is too hot
his insides explode
burning his dreams to ash

only the pilot light burns
in the stove of her belly

her process is cooling down

hers is the too-cold of side-stepping attack
getting out of the range of fire
not wanting hot tears to scald her cool skin ever again

O Queen of Cool
I name her

you skirt
the land of rage
preferring to walk in calmer
pastures

in your children's nightmares
you frolic with friends
in the meadow
while they pick their way through
yards of broken glass

trained in retreat
you live in the embroidered tent
of the dry-eyed

your mother is in there
never having made a canoe
of tears
to float *her* mother
to the other side

the poet of relearning-the-alphabet lives there
against her will
waiting to deliver her ribbon of words
to a flock of students in St Cloud
her tear ducts stopped

Protestant grandmothers are in there
lessons well learned
lift not thine hand in anger
speak only when spoken to

their corsets strain against bellows of grief

each paces with her psalter book
trailed close
by a starving shadow

only the shadow goes back and forth
across the border of night

borders of politeness
border of comfort
border of sanity
border of sorrow

there is a safety factor

you remain cool
to protect children from misplaced
rage of warriors
a cool cauldron for quenching

Is *this* my war?

in dreams I walk across no-man's land
bare-breasted

the distance between us, barren

an on-looker tells me it's courage
but it was only natural

dream

When the gang of men crawls in to the bunk room they are on all fours but huge and threatening. Their brawny, red t-shirted leader demands a certain number of our men and women. I freeze inside. My leader reacts without missing a beat: "the mothers do not go," waving me away. He randomly points to the ones who do have to go.

    mother turns to ice
    needles of frost creep into her veins
    spreading their anesthesia
    along her shelf-stacked spine

    fear contracts her
    hard   flat   angular
    dependent

    and the leader? What was he like?
    the dreamworker asks

Secure. One foot tucked under him on the bunk bed

looking down at the conqueror, I see
he's clearly capable of acting swiftly
In the heat of the moment he moves, she freezes..

old advice slips into the emptying mind of the dreamer
    give a little
                  get a little

silly & sing-song til she flares into rage
sending one more recruit
to the red-shirts

sisters shout instruction:
    bare your self to wrath!

If great grandmother had been able
to slash her bodice to ribbons
it might have saved her wrists

her daughter might have learned to live

my mother's bright plumage
might not have turned dull
out-of-season

she might have known why
she can not cry. Grief
after all

is the enemy
of war

stories shrouded by flattened affect
fall into dust behind the couch

I pick up the phone to check the facts
on my own life
reaching toward a definition of maturity
handed down in the roots
left dangling

maturus   knows the favorable moment for crossing
like the full red sun
at dawn
when a family's ancestral spirits
are recognized & praised

to go somewhere
wise
to where others who claim you
have been

Catastrophic interruption: a thought swerve crossing the Mississippi

NPR radio reports significant new finding off the coast of the US between
Florida and the Yucatan. Scientists have pulled up a 65 million-year-old core
of sediment from the ocean floor layered in such a way that it's possible to
read what happened when the 6-mile-wide meteorite smashed into Earth.

Like the scene in Fantasia *the dinosaurs broiled first. Hot iron sizzled through the earth's atmosphere raising the temperature furnace high. Then they froze (smoke blotted out the sun). After that ... a layer of nothing. "It's like it nuked the Earth."*

fire, ice, & darkness

dawn of the "Twilight Zone"

Episode: As the earth revolves closer to the sun, a woman
in her New York apartment struggles in a drenching fever, it's
getting hotter & hotter. She collapses at the door of an empty
refrigerator, no ice. Thugs
loot for water & the doctors can give her nothing to cool her
delirium.
When she wakes the room is covered in frost,
the doctors are bundled against a stove that's out of gas, no heat.
She's dying of cold as the earth spins
farther away from the sun.

Would you rather die of the heat
or the cold?

cold
specifically in the cold of her blue eye

its radiant ice shone
on the table linen

a photographer's white shield perfectly positioned
to glorify her face
except that lines of sorrow
remain in the air between us
in this restaurant called Ladies Happiness
                    Gedimino 31
                         Vilnius, Lithuania

strands of iron clad memory
wrought in the war years
never included me
yet
one end of sorrow's web
fastens to my lashes

on the verge of tears
we laugh
and rock too hard for flimsy chairs

it's because of you
fierce blue woman
with cigarette burning red
smoke rising behind you

posessed one moment by the battle whelp of Gediminas
in the next
on your knees at the Gate of Dawn
pitched to receive
the eternal tear
inscribed on the cheek of the Virgin

because we could lean into manliness
hidden in each other's arms

or because we could sing drinking songs together
rowdy as they are in love and war

comrade on the Beauty Way

because of you
     it began to happen
as never before in the history of Man

          the ice began to melt

dream

*A thousand men overboard throw ice and snow past the point of anger. They
are frenzied, aimless—constructing a playing field on a ship of ice. Hurtlers of
frozen projectiles, they spin like fuming grenades. Women and children get hit
with flying particles. We scream STOP when they hit Agla. "Sink their ship!"
I cry, and lead the attack. "Destroy their destroyer!" We all jump at once. It
sinks. Except for one part—still titanic like an iceberg on the back of a giant's
oxcart. We all sit on it together. A man laments the tragedy. This was to have
been the final model, christened with the names of the grandsons, built to last
forever.*

          words forced out
          through chutes of gravel
          scrape the sides of his throat

it tries to close
on the unprecedented
opening

a man apologizes

saying he regrets

his part

in all of this

centuries of sadness fill her dry hollow
choking from the belly up
on grief's long tale

she is finally moved
to tears

the gentle man
touches her arm
         don't cry like that

it's the only way I know how

  awakened
   in a quiet room
by my own cries
it is still Lithuania. It is freezing

a sun has indeed risen
its light largely blocked
by upright slabs
of Soviet construction—
housing for the untouchables,
Russians cleared out of Moscow
before the Olympics

exposed walls
misfit windows
a constant exchange
of cold air
braces sleepers
for dawn

in this gradual morning
I realize I am inside a gray building
staring out a curtained eye

envying the chilled clarity
of a people who know
for dead sure
who the enemy is

protected by billowing warmth
of laughter & mid-night song
filling this very room

I spent the night with ice & iron
to discover their ancient smiths
chained the sun into the sky

it stares
down into earth's swamp-hole
where the devil hides
and dwarfs dig for ore
concealed
in her horrible O

She-swamp guards her black O
with musty brown grasses
& bubbling mud

storm wet ooze
& ravaged debris

her muck
a palette for animals
whose tracks
score music
in slime

next to birdfoot runes
determined prints of small
possibly human
feet
lead somewhere
vastly interior

invisible
to Sun at the height
of his power

aged-ones
in cramped bodies
travel undetected

crafty swamp men
moving in & out of Mother
made rich by her ability to keep
secrets

his pick in her vein
the dwarf keeps a finger on our pulse
tap-tapping his way along a dank corridor
                         of greed let's say
                         or shame
                 he gathers what we mean
                     even when we don't say it
                 storing it up in piles that petrify
                     or age into gems

nonplussed guardian of the perilous passage
    unlike us
        he has all the time in the world
                geological time
            action packed solid   in   molten slo-mo dwarfs
            shovel, pick, dig, divert, stack, channel, forge, hide

we could call them
pattern-keepers
who know the technical manual by heart
  so many parts fire
   to so many parts water

to conjoin the relevant twins

     resistance & resilience
   as perSIST is to SALLY
       leaping in exile
       exulting
        insulting

the ancient energies of
Take-a-stand & Rise-again

twine in gnarly roots of folk who stood their ground
when the tanks came through
& again
at the shrine of Kryziu Kolnas
when the gray machines
more than once
leveled the Hill of Crosses

bulldozers rolled
towards the pilgrim tokens

thousands upon thousands of crosses
wrought carved cast
festooned with flags

crissed with antennae
crossed with moons
snake rods rising high on the hill
spiral vanes
wing-tipped & tuning a galvanized sky

who did they force to drive
into that radiant field
and what did he
pray
tell
in the weird morning
when
after dire wreckage
the iron crosses
stood
again
as if forced up
from
below

V
WAR'S PLANET

Wanting to fly over her own life like Beryl the bush pilot with a notepad and quiver of pencils strapped to her thigh, the poet notes that the body of woman has become a casualty of war. Miss America is five pounds thinner every year and still losing. The parade of women's styles is everywhere affected by the military. Yet Athena was nowhere to be heard at the meeting with concerned citizens and an army general, peace time conversion issues on the table. Hephaistos strikes while the iron is hot. The poet loses her voice until she gets the instructions for the furnace dance which is a necessity at the end of a millennium.

Approaching the year 2000
on fashion's runway
the manacled body of woman
spiked & chained

is no more strange
than the waifs we were

occupying coffee bars
in camouflage & epaulets

or last week talking
with our husbands & the ex
four-star general

wives in trim suits
shoulder pads & frowns

bone-thin women
turn their backs
float their flesh
hip to hip
swivel lithe
& turn
blue-shaded sockets
as empty above
as links in the chain below

press into flesh

bound
by history
to

RE   she cranes her neck to read the letters

PEAT   written in black above

RE

NEW

repeat or renew: divine injunction chafes the brain
sign that the armored one wants out
her javelin scrapes into the crown of god's skull
steel jabs bone

the mind in the mind of god
readies her grey-green eyes
fastens helmet
ties sandals
crouches in wait

a dark sound
rude as the first contraction
gathers in the distance
  the patriarchal brow twists
     sensing Releaser coming

its guttural thunder travels up the scale
with urgent rasp & pant of a pianist pounding
precisely
home
   clong!
   k-pow!
   ka-kling!

observers disagree over
which iron mallet
 (of a swarthy armed hero)
cracked
the head of Zeus

but they all say
—SHE emerged
splendid
fully armed
instantly able to return his gaze

Athena posed as her own model on Big Daddy's runway

this one will never be a wife

she stopped mid-stride
to lay her javelin down
undid metallic girdle
removed helmet
placed shield
on peeling dirt

just as her hand lifted the pin
to undo her dress
she was surrounded by African sisters
daubed in Triton's river mud
red-stripped goatskins swirling
a wild thicket of women browned
& blood-proud
made a shield of themselves
to protect her sharp nakedness

a brand new royal girl

the wild sisters led her
into silver water

they immersed her by degrees & smooth
til numberless tongues had coolly lapped away
all effluence of father

shout circles
laugh circles
encompass her
the woman circle cleanses her
cup their hands to drum the water
da doomp da doomp
da doomp doomp m doomp
deep-toned sparkles splash high
& flash
a glistening curtain curls apart

RE BORN!

as Ht Nt they welcomed her
as Ath Neit they welcomed her
as A-ta-na they welcomed her

all things began to wake
coals in the pan stirred
the oil press creaked
wing feathers lifted
water in the calabash rippled
wool unwound
spines arched
spears & all manner of implements for war
registered slow thrill moving up their shafts

the promise of action

wherever she walked

beauty in the order of things shifted into the present

elements align themselves
clouds march in formation
seven colors beginning with red
line up (half a halo) over fields of diamond grass

coiled serpents fly straight
& birds with woman faces
croak oracular prose

scraps of paper on the writer's desk arrange themselves
distraction narrows to focus
tools become intelligent

extraordinary marriages occur:
image engages strategy
bliss takes the hand of precision

Dear N

When I am about to get hit by vision I dream about you.
Often you and Charles are talking (sometimes even exclude
me... so much for ego) right before there is an "opening"
and I am possessed by mythological vision. Charles takes
the role of Hermes and you are my Athena. All I know is
that there are archetypal roles to be played and we draft

friends and acquaintances to play them... My task right
now is to learn to clean up and finish my work, to break
things down into units...the Hephaistos "stuff," and in-
cidentally my feet are getting better the more I keep my
nose to the grindstone—or is it focus to the forge? Any-
way that nasty old smith god just keeps forging me, feet
to the fire.

Andrea

caught in her dream
points of a polished mind
shine

the poet wanted
to be seen in blossom
profuse
 a vessel of golden honey

growing up the grey warrior
isn't sexy
which doesn't matter before the age of 12
when the Parrier, the Plotter, and tom-boy Pallas
direct traffic in a girl's imagination

She-of-the-wisest-counsel
does not employ erotic fantasy
to get her work done

it's fine for everyone else
but

ask Hephaistos

who tried to strike while his iron was hot

brushing him off she says
I come
for new armor

his greatest admirer!
who would not trust the divine contours of her body
to any other designer

above all
she chooses him for the skill in his hands

his feel for the flame

animateur of
inanimate things

I am in the moment with Homer
noting the space of silence
in which thought prepares itself

looking up from our respective chairs
across the years
our lines of diffuse sight go off like roads
in different directions

in this mirror I know what thinking looks like

break a task down into bits
he advised
send postcards home
pre-addressed
an idea at a time
you'll have your own report
waiting at your door

& so I suppose a scribe was conceived
notebooks in hand
at basketball games
in the choir stall
at the opera
even at the campsite with father
    I took notes on chaos theory by firelight

last month
going home to help re-organize
for the onslaught of age
I came back with a note
scratched on the back of a drugstore receipt

        Fe" (2)   reduced form
           ferrous   in vegetables

        Fe'" (3)   oxidized form
           ferric   blast furnace
                                 meteor
      Fe (304)
           or (203)   mixtures
                    for cave painting   walls
                       cosmetics?

red-ochre rust to brown
abundant crusting surface stuffs
hematite limonite goethite
heated cherts & chalcedonies
powders spread & airblown rouge
reduced to iron blacke&darke&foule
burnt out dross of smelted slag
salamander bear & bloom

listen

Homo Faber
man the maker & your hot god
Ignis Divinus
who some think is Christ the Divine Blacksmith

There is always a woman in the fire.

the one I am about to speak of
carries rouge in a shin bone

kiss of Ogun
rust
mixed with fat of an animal

at dusk she finds the spot

tilts to the nauseate angle
of god's rod
stuck in the ground
a surveyor's mark
sensitive to which side you're on

already a slight buzzing in her head
eyes whirl
tongue thickens

mama mambo lo
bends straight from the waist
red dots on her out-stretched fingers
earth licks them clean

she exhales
on smudge
snapping adder-spats of flame
into fire

from above the scene resembles a tight spiral
    circle of grass
            orange fire basin
                    beaded forearm laid across a drum

mambo's spin slows to the node of her feet
fixed & rooting
down
& down
to the throbbing vein

struck
& jolted then
ore power pulses up her bones
to lodge in a shoulder blade

with terrible speed
she wheels into work
wing juts thrusting
hip gears greased to roll

her flat foot
slaps the ground
reeling one way
& back
entranced
but on alert
for an exact signal

site the smelter here
or it will never sing!

alchemists in loud agreement
say the furnace will be dumb
& all its products stillborn
unless it be placed exactly between the voices of people
& the voice of the ore

can you hear it?

my old professor stops mid-way on the path winding out to sea

delicate grasses
crystal sea
we walk alone on flattened cones of sand

he turns back toward route 1

can you hear it?

I can just barely hear
civilization streaming by in a train of sound

on the other side soundless surf
hits the cliff

I can't hear it

both horizons vast
engineered curve of coastal road
& sun-spillt sweep of sea

he stops once more to rest his question on the wind

it slaps back at my cheek

Can you hear it?

caught between two conversations
explorers on the brink
of the millennium

eyes wet
stomach swooping

a dowser feels it in his stomach
an elderly neighbor on the East coast says

the neighbor on the other side
stands up on his morning deck
in khaki clothes and skin
I imagine he watches a fisherman
but he's rigid in salute
to Old Glory inching up a pole

which flag will you chose to carry you over?

how many hands do I have?

her banner drips
sea rain
azure beads   silver spangles

wetness is her weapon

another banner bursts with sequins
red & gold
waving a black fist

we are told just in time
that Mars has moisture in its field
red dust *and* water
a brilliant blue V
over a setting sun

War's planet
an exquisite desolation
worth a thousand years of words

the manned space station must
take more pictures
leave no litter

when the house burns down
save the photos

O Lord of our Fathers
on your fiery way out

Victory is having something left to give

About the Author

Nor Hall is a psychotherapist, imaginal scholar and theatre-collaborator. She did anthropology at Beloit College and received her PhD. in the History of Consciousness from the University of California, Santa Cruz. Her books include *The Moon and the Virgin: Images of the Archetypal Feminine*, *Broodmales*, *Those Women*. For the last ten years she has worked with Pantheatre (Paris) and Archipelago Theatre (Chapel Hill) in the development of new pieces that give archetypal work a stage. Several of her articles have appeared in the *Spring Journal*: on Jess and Robert Duncan (*Dreamway* 59) and the "Architecture of Intimacy" (*Marriages* 60). She and her husband live happily on either sides of the Mississippi anchoring an extended family in Minnesota.